PAWNBROKING

An Aspect of
British Social History

KENNETH HUDSON

Pawnbroking

An Aspect of
British Social History

THE BODLEY HEAD
LONDON   SYDNEY
TORONTO

British library Cataloguing
in Publication Data
Hudson, Kenneth
Pawnbroking: an aspect of
British social history
1. Pawnbroking –
Great Britain – History
I. Title
332.3'4   HG2085.G/
ISBN: 0–370–30447–0

© Kenneth Hudson 1982
Printed in Great Britain for
The Bodley Head Ltd
9 Bow Street, London, WC2E 7AL
by Redwood Burn Ltd, Trowbridge
set in Monotype Imprint
by Gloucester Typesetting Services
First published 1982

CONTENTS

Acknowledgments, 6

List of illustrations, 7

Preface, 9

1. The Silence of the Historians, 13

2. Pawning in Pre-industrial Times, 21

3. The Georgian and Early Victorian Pawnbrokers:
   Problems and Opportunities, 35

4. From the Great Exhibition to the
   Death of Queen Victoria, 53

5. The Early Twentieth Century, 75

6. The Inter-war Years and the Great Depression, 97

7. Pawnbroking in the Age of Social Security
   and the Welfare State, 120

8. A Future for Pawnbroking?, 137

Appendices, 150

Books and articles relating to pawnbroking, 160

ACKNOWLEDGMENTS

More than three hundred people have helped me in the preparation of this book by contributing their personal memories of pawnbroking. Many of them have most trustingly lent photographs and documents which have been an invaluable additional source of information. I am most grateful to them all for their kindness and for the time they have devoted to answering my numerous questions. Without their first-hand knowledge of yesterday's pawnbroking, this book would not have been possible.

I owe a special debt of gratitude to John Cook of Bristol, who eased the planning of the book through a number of difficult stages in an admirably diplomatic manner and built bridges between myself and the National Pawnbrokers' Association which have stood the test of time.

I am also greatly indebted to the General Secretary of the Association, Jack Brown, whose unequalled knowledge of the trade and its personalities over more than half a century has made my task so much easier and more rewarding, and who guided me through the Association's archives in such an exemplary fashion. My warmest thanks are also due to the Association itself, which has given the most generous support to the publication of this book and to the research which preceded it.

List of Illustrations

1 'Gin Lane' by William Hogarth, 1751: the first known representation of a British pawnbroker's shop (*left*)
2 An East End pawnshop, as seen by *The Illustrated London News*, 1886. (Illustrated London News Picture Library)
3 Outside a pawn office at Merthyr Tydfil, 1875. (Illustrated London News Picture Library)
4 Saturday night at a London pawnbroker's, 1906. (From George R. Sims (ed.), *Living London*, Cassell, 1906)
5 The furniture room in a London pawnbroker's warehouse, 1906. (From George R. Sims (ed.), *Living London*, Cassell, 1906)
6 A London pawnbroker's store, 1906: storing bundles in the weekly pledge room. (From George R. Sims (ed.), *Living London*, Cassell, 1906)
7 Burns's pawnshop, Millwood and Clayton Streets, Glasgow, 1926. (Mitchell Library, Glasgow)
8 A sale of unredeemed goods at Debenham, Storr and Co., London, 1906. (From George R. Sims (ed.), *Living London*, Cassell, 1906)
9 Parker's, Middlewood Road, Sheffield, c. 1920. (W. J. Parker)
10 Sir John Swaish as Lord Mayor of Bristol. (J. D. G. Cook)
11 The Council of the National Pawnbrokers' Association, early 1920s. The President, Walter Bull, is in the front row, second from the left, and the Honorary Secretary, F. K. Ohlson, is on his left. (NPA)
12 Belfast pawnbrokers' outing, 1930. At that time there were ninety pawnbrokers' shops in Belfast, and consequently plenty of scope for social activities. (John Nicholson)
13 G. W. Thomson, 234 Praed Street, London, c. 1912. Mr H. W. Mobbs, the manager, then aged 24, is in the doorway. (G. H. Mobbs)
14 The Board Room at the headquarters of the National Pawnbrokers' Association, with painting of Walter Bull above the fireplace. (NPA)
15 Interior of T. M. Sutton's shop, Victoria, c. 1939. (T. M. Sutton Ltd)
16 Catalogue of auction of forfeited pledges, Frederick T. Clamp, Nottingham, 1936 (cover). (J. T. Herring)
17 Contract issued by T. M. Sutton Ltd, 156 Victoria Street, London s.w.1. (T. M. Sutton Ltd)

18 Clamp's auction catalogue, 1936: sample page, showing prices realised. (J. T. Herring)
19 Licence issued to A. D. and J. D. Cook of Bristol, 1976. (J. D. G. Cook)
20 Exterior of Harvey & Thompson's new shop in Golders Green, which has no retail department. (J. D. Taylor)
21 Interior of Harvey & Thompson's new shop, showing pledging counter. (J. D. Taylor)
22 Modern interior of W. Taylor's shop in Nottingham, showing type and quality of goods for sale. (J. T. Herring)

PREFACE

This is the first general study of British pawnbroking to have been published since 1892.* For reasons I do not fully understand the subject has been virtually ignored by social historians, pushed off the stage as if it were obscene. Yet until very recently the pawnshop was of great, even crucial importance to working-class people all over the British Isles. For generation after generation of poor families, life, before the coming of the Welfare State, was difficult enough: without the local pawnbroker it would often have been impossible.

On the whole, 'Uncle' has not had a good press. Journalists, especially in London, have usually portrayed him as a shifty, dishonest character, the friend of thieves and rogues, and almost certainly Jewish. Novelists have followed the same pattern. The reality is very different: as a class, there can have been few more solid, law-abiding people than pawnbrokers, not infrequently respectable and conservative to the point of tediousness. If there is a valid criticism of nineteenth- and twentieth-century pawnbrokers it is not that they have been unscrupulous rascals, profitably preying on society, but that they have shown themselves so anxious to be thought well of by society, so determined to behave as other worthy and successful businessmen do. A little more adventurousness and originality would often have been welcome. The photographs of pawnbrokers included in the present book are those of churchgoing tradesmen, not of pirates.

* Alfred Hardaker, *A Brief History of Pawnbroking*. This book, however, was concerned mainly with the circumstances leading up to the 1872 Pawnbrokers' Act and with the campaign to get it through Parliament.

9

What is being attempted in the following pages, therefore, is to show the British pawnbroker as he really is and has been, and to assess his social and economic role from the eighteenth century to the present day. In order to do this effectively, it has been necessary to say something about the development of pledging during previous centuries, against a background of religious hostility and fluctuating persecution. The British seem always to have had a love-hate relationship with their pawnbrokers. They have needed them and appreciated their services, and, at the same time, experienced strong feelings of guilt about requiring this form of credit. A mortgage or a bank loan are matters one can discuss with one's friends; but a loan from a pawnbroker is something most people have preferred to conceal. The roots of this interesting and significant difference of attitude are to be found in the history of the two kinds of borrowing. Mortgages and bank loans have been associated with the middle and upper classes, but what the pawnshop has traditionally provided is, for the most part, money for the hard-up members of the working class. To be known to pawn has been to confess oneself *déclassé*, and in a class-ridden society like ours that has been something almost too dreadful to contemplate.

In carrying out research for the book, much use has been made of the reminiscences of pawnbrokers and their customers. They have been asked a wide range of questions about their personal experiences of the trade and their replies constitute a body of information which is of considerable social and historical importance. Because of this evidence – oral history – the twentieth century is much more fully and satisfactorily documented than the years which preceded it. Time and again one longs for first-hand evidence from the eighteenth and nineteenth centuries, evidence which simply does not exist, and one knows, in consequence, that many of one's comments and generalisations are not as soundly based as one would have wished. Without the voices of the people who have been personally involved, who have helped to make it, the writing of history is a dangerous exercise.

Pawnbroking at the moment is in a critical phase. The old days of pawning bedding, clothes and the tools of one's trade have clearly gone, probably for ever, and the local pawnshop which was at the centre of this way of life has vanished with it. The Social Security office has taken over the job. But meanwhile quite a different type of pawnbroking has been developing under the skin of the old one. During thirty years of what, for millions of people, has been unprecedented affluence, life styles and social expectations have undergone fundamental changes. One curiously ignored aspect of the process of spreading wealth thinner has been that the kind of objects which interest the pawnbroker nowadays, jewellery and other articles on which he can safely lend fifty pounds and more, are now, like mortgages, cars, electrical appliances and foreign holidays, to be found in millions, instead of thousands of homes. With a new standard of living to maintain at all costs and with a stock of valuables which can be pledged to raise cash, today's ex-poor or new rich, however one chooses to define them, are ready-made customers for the pawnbroker who knows how to attract them. The old techniques, the old premises, the old kind of staff and the old brand of personal relationships simply will not work. Today's borrowers or potential borrowers have no wish to visit places which make them feel that they are going down in the world. Having climbed, they not unnaturally want to stay there.

A fairly high proportion of what we might call the new pledgers are not, for various reasons, very likely to qualify for bank loans and, in any case, they might well find the procedure involved rather forbidding. The idea of instant money on the security of what is tangibly and obviously their own property can be more attractive. One is, as it were, claiming a right, not begging a favour, and, since a high proportion of the nation's jewellery belongs to women, the right kind of pawnbroker can be made to seem a very feminist institution, catering for women in their own right, not as mere legal appendages to their husbands.

It is a reasonable assessment of the situation that we are now in the early stages of a radical re-grouping, reorganisation and re-presentation of the pawnbroking business. The need is there, the customers are there, and the finance is there. All that has so far been lacking is an imaginative and carefully planned public relations effort to blow the spark into flame. For nearly a hundred years the National Pawnbrokers' Association has devoted most of its efforts to convincing the public at large that pawnbrokers are decent, hardworking, law-abiding businessmen and to protecting its members against people who in one way or another have been trying to defraud them. It seems very likely that what will be mainly required of the Association during the next ten years will be that it shall transform itself into a primarily public relations body, to bring the new pawnbrokers into contact with the new potential customers.

I

The Silence of the Historians

The British pawnbroker can fairly claim to have had a raw deal from the historians. They have not so much misrepresented him as almost totally ignored him. A careful search through the numerous social and economic histories of Britain published during the past fifty years reveals hardly a trace of someone who was a central figure in working-class life for more than two centuries, a person without whom millions of poor families would have starved and been evicted from their homes for the lack of money to pay the rent. His nickname, 'Uncle', is surely significant. He was the friendly neighbourhood figure to whom his hard-up nephews and nieces could always turn for advice and a loan, the solid leaning-post in times of weakness and trouble. Yet, vitally important as he once was to the working-class economy, until a combination of social forces – war, full employment, hire-purchase and the Welfare State – pushed him somewhat brusquely and ungratefully into the background, he has been quite remarkably little studied and written about.

In his pioneering and immensely successful *English Social History: a Survey of Six Centuries, Chaucer to Queen Victoria*, first published in 1942, a time when most theories, taboos and attitudes were in the melting pot, G. M. Trevelyan does not mention pawnbroking once from cover to cover, although it is precisely the kind of subject that one might have expected to interest him. Social history he defines as 'the history of a people with the politics left out', and he goes on to observe, quite rightly, that the links between economic and social history are necessarily and fruitfully very close. 'For,' he insists, 'the social scene grows out of economic conditions, to much the same extent that political events in their turn grow out of social conditions. Without social history, economic history is barren and political history is unintelligible.'[1]

Trevelyan goes on to explain the scope of social history, as he saw it. It was nothing more or less, he said, than 'the daily life of the inhabitants of the land in past ages', and this included 'the human as well as the economic relation of different classes to one another, the character of family and household life, the attitude of man to nature, the culture of each age as it arose out of these general conditions of life'.[2]

And from all this the pawnshop, the people's banker for so many generations, becomes curiously locked out. Borrowing money, for Trevelyan as for other historians, seems always to have been something which concerned exclusively the rich and powerful. It has had, if one were to rely on Trevelyan's evidence, nothing whatever to do with the lower orders. Princes and merchants might raise money on loan; the labouring poor belonged to an altogether different level or species of humanity which never came into contact with finance. So, in *English Social History*, we can read a good deal about royal borrowings from Jewish financiers and Florentine merchants, about the high interest rates the monastic houses had to suffer at the hands of the Italian and English moneylenders, about the goldsmiths' function as 'proto-bankers' in the seventeenth century, about the highly respectable banking skills of the Quakers in the early nineteenth. But the words 'pawnshop' and 'pawnbroker' are never mentioned at all. The nearest we get to them is a mysterious and unhelpful reference to the emergence in late Georgian times of 'a low type of Hebrew moneylender . . . abhorred not without reason by his victims, the impecunious and unthrifty of all classes'.[3]

The reason why Trevelyan has nothing to say about the pawnshop is unlikely to be either prejudice or squeamishness. On the contrary, he rather enjoys writing about what used to be called 'low life'. He devotes, for example, several pages to the rise and fall of gin-drinking and to the effects of cheap gin on the death rate of the working classes, and he refers to 'Hogarth's famous delineation of the horrors of Gin Lane', without mentioning the fact that a quarter of the picture is taken up by the premises of 'S. Gripe, Pawnbroker', complete with the famous three balls hanging above the door. Here is the carpenter offering the pawnbroker his saw, without which he would be unable to earn a living, and the housewife her kettle and cauldron, in order to convert the proceeds into gin, and there, opposite the pawnshop, is 'Kilman, Distiller', ready and waiting to supply all comers. Yet Trevelyan concentrates exclusively on the gin. It is very curious. What was it about pawnbroking that made it unfit for an historian's attention, irrelevant?

The most probable answer is that until very recently historians carried out their research entirely in libraries. This worked greatly to the disadvantage of humble people, that is, of the bulk of the population, since no scholar went out of his way to make their acquaintance and to listen to them talking about their lives. The odd social reformer might choose to do so; magistrates, of necessity, were made aware of at least some of the habits and beliefs of the masses; the exceptional novelist might consider it professionally useful to do a little slumming, and from time to time a Parliamentary Enquiry or a Royal Commission could decide to take evidence directly from people whose voices were otherwise extremely unlikely to be heard outside their own milieu.

If Trevelyan had had the time and the inclination to move about urban Britain collecting the views and memories of the poor, he could hardly have escaped hearing about pawnbroking several times a day. He would have had other surprises as well, of course, and he might well have felt obliged to modify the contents and the balance of his book as a result. But since, like practically every other historian of his day, he carried out his researches entirely among printed material, supplemented by conversations with colleagues and friends and to a very small extent by pictures, the problem did not arise.

This is in no way intended as a criticism of Trevelyan, merely to indicate that he belonged to his age and that his work had the limitations which followed from that. Trevelyan made social history respectable, an immense achievement, and in consequence prepared the way for a new generation of researchers and writers who saw the possibilities of previously neglected and untapped sources of information, who were motorised and who were able to use tools, notably the tape-recorder and the photocopying machine, which were unknown to their predecessors. It would be a slight exaggeration to say that tape-recording and xeroxing have rescued the pawnbroker from undeserved oblivion, but with such a large amount of new material to be discovered and organised, I myself would certainly have found it difficult to collect and file my evidence without these two great time-savers.

Perhaps the oddest feature of this pawnbroking blackout is the almost total silence on the part of those writers who have set out, deliberately and outspokenly, to tell the story of the British working class. E. P. Thompson, in his long and influential book, *The Making of the English Working Class*, published in 1963, offers us not even a passing reference to the pawnshop and its place within the nineteenth-century urban community. Nor do those equally committed historians of a slightly earlier period, G. D. H. Cole and Raymond Postgate, in *The Common People, 1746–1938*, despite the mass of valuable details they provide about wages, unemployment, 'castes, taboos, commercial methods and social habits'. The Pawnbrokers' Acts of 1764 and 1872, which were of great importance to the working classes, are not included in the six pages of 'important dates' which are given as an appendix to the book, although the Battle of Culloden, the introduction of income tax, Darwin's *Origin of Species* and Daimler's engine are all here, despite their somewhat indirect links with the lives and habits of the British working class.

The authors of *The Making of the English Working Class* and *The Common People* – these two books have been taken as examples mainly because they have been particularly well known and much quoted – were, after all, academic historians responsible for successful and authoritative works. They were, one could say without the slightest intention to offend, library people whose strong political motivations caused them to concentrate on working-class history. They would certainly have made no claim to be 'oral historians', that is, scholars whose primary research material includes the first-hand experiences of men and women of all classes who have been directly involved in historical events and processes.

The case of George Orwell is rather different. Although, like Thompson, Cole and Postgate, he had a middle-class background, he deliberately lived, for journalistic reasons, among working-class people in the early and mid Thirties. He had an enquiring mind, a sharp eye and, unfashionably, a keen and discriminating sense of smell. His two books, *Down and Out in Paris and London* (1933) and *The Road to Wigan Pier* (1937) showed what it was like to have to exist on the typical income of a working-class family during the dreadful years of the inter-war depression. Unlike many other writers of his time, Orwell was neither a Communist nor a fellow-traveller. He was an independent, objective observer and he described exactly what he saw, heard, smelt, tasted and felt during his journeying through the industrial areas of Britain. He reports on budgets, health, living conditions, diets, rents, gambling, entertainment, clothes – but he never mentions the pawnbroker. Neither, equally strangely, does J. B. Priestley, whose accounts of England in the Thirties were shrewdly observed, honestly written and very popular.

Both Priestley and Orwell must have talked to hundreds of people who used pawnshops, or who knew many people who did, and they both prided themselves on being men who called a spade a spade. I myself have hundreds of statements from men and women whose families made ends meet during the Twenties and Thirties by means of regular visits to the pawnbroker. I have no reason to believe that my contacts are any better than those of these two writers, but it has been made clear to me beyond any possible doubt that during the period with which they were concerned the pawnshop was central to the lives of the poorer sections of the community, at least in towns. Why, then, do such socially-minded, responsible, crusading writers as Priestley and Orwell have nothing to say about pawnbrokers and pawnshops?

The most likely explanation – it is difficult to think of any other – is that pawning was something that poor people preferred not to discuss with outsiders. Among their friends and neighbours, in their own immediate community, pawning, like sex, was a fact of life. There was no need to mention it. One knew, one accepted it. But with strangers it was quite a different matter. Strangers would not understand. They would be unable to see pawnbroking in its proper context, to grasp how it fitted into family life. To somebody with whom one had not grown up, who had different values and experiences from oneself, the fact that one went to the pawnshop might suggest that one was a poor manager, feckless, a spendthrift, none of which were necessarily true at all. So, in order to preserve one's pride and integrity, it was much better to keep quiet. If Orwell and Priestley had asked them directly, 'Do you go to the pawnshop?' they might possibly have dissembled, although I think they would have been rather more likely to give a truthful, if not chatty, answer. But if the question was never put to them at all, as apparently it was not, why should they volunteer the information?

Only now, after so many people have unlocked their memories for me, can I see what an extraordinary situation this was. Here was a social custom which had been widespread for generations and which nobody talked or wrote about, except when pawnbroking, for one reason or another, happened to attract the attention of the police and the courts. In general, one supposes, pawnbroking was simply not felt to be interesting. I know of no other significant aspect of British society which has been so consistently ignored by those who make a living by reflecting, analysing and criticising that society. The pawnbrokers knew, their customers knew, but very few other people seem to have done. As with homosexuality, there was what amounted to a conspiracy of silence. These were matters one preferred not to discuss with outsiders.

Even for those people who were interested and who wanted to learn more about pawnbroking, there was and is very little that a library or a bookshop could offer, apart from articles in encyclopaedias and learned journals. The only books with any claim to be standard works were both published a long time ago, Hardaker's *A Brief History of Pawnbroking* in 1892 and Levine's *The Business of Pawnbroking* in 1913. There is nothing which covers the Twenties and Thirties, one of the most important periods in the history of British pawnbroking.

In all these circumstances, it is hardly surprising that what we might term the non-pawning public should know so little of what really happens in the trade, that myths and prejudices about it should be so abundant, and that the stereotype of the pawnbroker should be so ludicrously wrong. If one talks, as I have, to a fairly wide cross-section of the British public, one finds a general belief that most pawnbrokers are Jewish, that they charge extortionate rates of interest, that they are all receivers of stolen property on a large scale, that their premises are dark, filthy and up back alleys, and that once an article has been pawned one has very little chance of ever getting it back. To bring this image up to date and closer to reality is one of the main purposes of the present book.

The best-known description of a pawnshop in the English language is by Charles Dickens in *Sketches by Boz*.[4] Since it first appeared nearly 150 years ago, it has conditioned, directly and indirectly, the attitude of generation after generation of British people towards the pawnbroker and his trade. What Dickens described in such picturesque terms is what most of our fellow-countrymen, including, of course, journalists, playwrights and film and television producers, expect a pawnshop to be like. However inaccurate the picture may be nowadays, however melodramatic, distorted and unfair it may have been in Dickens's own day, this is what the public wants to believe and it has the great novelist's enormous prestige to set it on its way and give it stamina.

Nothing could have been more damning than the first few lines of Dickens's essay. 'Of all the numerous receptacles for misery and distress with which the streets of London unhappily abound,' he wrote, 'there are perhaps none which present such striking scenes of vice and poverty as the pawnbrokers' shops. The very nature of these places occasions their being but little known, except to the unfortunate beings whose profligacy or misfortune drives them to seek the temporary relief they offer.' The shop is 'low, dirty-looking, dusty', the adjoining houses 'straggling, shrunken and rotten', the unredeemed pledges in the window unattractive and of small value. The customers include a prostitute and a man with an 'inflamed countenance and drunken stagger', an ill-tempered brute who beats and kicks his wife, 'a wretched worn-out woman in the last stages of consumption'. The pawnbroker is an 'elegantly attired individual', with 'curly black hair, diamond ring and double silver watch-guard', who treats his customers with the greatest lack of consideration and courtesy. It is small wonder that one hesitating customer, who has never entered a pawnshop before, 'looking cautiously round to ascertain that no one watches him, hastily slinks in'.

The picture is not a pleasant one. Dickens was unequalled as a presenter of low life and the more he pulled out the stops the more his middle-class readers loved it. But British society has changed a little since 1836 and one can well understand that today's pawnbrokers should resent the idea that Dickens would feel immediately at home in one of their shops, that their trade has marked time for 150 years.

NOTES

1 Introduction, vii.
2 Introduction, vii–viii.
3 page 395.
4 Chapter 23, page 1.

2

Pawning in Pre-industrial Times

It has been claimed, somewhat recklessly,[1] that the trade of the pawnbrokers existed in China 3,000 years ago, and that it was a familiar feature of daily life in the cities of classical Greece and Rome. 'The trade of the pawnbroker' evidently signifies different things to different people, and there is a great danger of applying a modern meaning to periods in the past when conditions were entirely different. The Chinese and the ancient Greeks may well have known the custom of lending money on the security of goods, but this is not necessarily the same as having the trade of the pawnbroker. It may well be that a Chinese or a Greek shopkeeper or merchant combined that function with lending money as and when such a service was required. But that does not make him a pawnbroker in the sense in which we understand the term today.

The well-known verses in *Deuteronomy* should undoubtedly be interpreted in a very general way.

'Thou shalt not lend money upon usury to thy brother; usury of money, usury of victuals, usury of anything that is lent upon usury.'[2]

'Unto a stranger thou mayest lend upon usury, but unto thy brother thou shalt not lend upon usury.'[3]

'No man shall take the nether or the upper millstone to pledge, for he taketh a man's life to pledge.'[4]

'When thou dost lend thy brother any thing, thou shalt not go into his house to fetch his pledge. Thou shalt stand abroad and the man to whom thou dost lend shall bring out the pledge abroad unto thee.'[5]

This refers to what one might call amateur pawning, to a transaction carried out between one individual and another. It does not imply that the person granting the loan was in business for that purpose, simply that he was behaving prudently by insisting on tangible security for the money he was lending. It may well be that certain members of the community were more inclined than others to make loans in this way, very probably because they had more money to lend, but that does not necessarily make them members of a trade.

We are always, to some extent, the prisoners of words, especially translated words, and what appears to be the same word may have had very different meanings in different periods and in different civilisations. Christ may have driven the moneylenders from the Temple, but on what scale their operations may have been and whether their moneylending was combined with other trading activities we have really very little idea. All that we can be sure of is that for thousands of years some people have been in the habit of borrowing and that others have had to find ways of protecting themselves against those who failed to pay the money back. Accepting pledges is no more than a sensible way of protecting oneself against defaulters.

There is no evidence as to whether pawnbroking, which is a business, a trade, was known in Roman Britain, although the habit of pledging assuredly was. The existence of anything similar to it is unrecorded among the Saxons and Danes after the collapse of Roman civilisation in Britain and, whatever may have been going on in China, so far as Western civilisation was concerned, pawnbroking as an activity in its own right becomes distinguishable only in the later Middle Ages, when it flourished primarily to meet the needs of powerful and ambitious rulers, who required money to finance wars and the building of castles, palaces and churches, and to maintain a standard of living which they considered appropriate to their rank, power and social position.

Medieval society depended on the belief that religion embraced and controlled all aspects of human life. Man was on earth, not in order to pursue his economic self-interest but to fulfil himself within a clearly recognised social structure. Each member of society had his own clearly defined function and station, as a priest or monk, as a soldier, as a merchant, or as a peasant. For each vocation there was an appropriate reward to which one was

22

entitled and it was wrong to ask for more. Society was held together by a system of mutual, but varying obligations. Lords
should not rob peasants. Craftsmen and merchants should receive
sufficient for their needs, but no more.

Such at least was the theory, but, inevitably, the practice, even
in Rome, was different. Moneymaking, 'money bringing money',
was to be found everywhere. As R. H. Tawney has said, 'The
Papacy might denounce usurers, but as the centre of the most
highly organised administrative system of the age, receiving remit-
tances from all over Europe, and receiving them in money at a
time when the revenue of other governments still included personal services and payments in kind, it could not dispense with
them.'[6] Matters got worse, not better, as time went on. Priests
engaged in trade. Cathedral chapters lent money at high rates of
interest. A moneylender was recommended by the Bishop of Paris
to devote his ill-gotten gains to the building of Notre Dame.

But throughout the Middle Ages the Church continued to regard
economic motives as suspect. The urge to make money was a
dangerous passion and, like the other passions, it had to be kept
under tight control. Trade was legitimate, but one had to be sure
that it was carried on for the public good. Private property was a
necessary institution, but it was to be tolerated as a concession to
human frailty, not pursued or praised as a good in itself. Prices
should be such as would allow each person to have the necessities
of life appropriate to his station, and no more. No one should
charge money for a loan, although he might demand compensation if the principal was not repaid at the date laid down.
There was no objection to rent or profit, provided they were
reasonable; what was condemned as immoral was a fixed and certain payment in respect of a loan or investment. To take such a
payment was usury, which was robbery and contrary to Scrip-
ture.

The peak of the ecclesiastical attack on usury was reached at the
Council of Lyon in 1274 and the Council of Vienna in 1312. These
confirmed the measures taken by the Third Lateran Council in
1175, but added to them new rules which made the moneylender
an outlaw, an enemy of society. No one was to let houses to usurers.
They were to be refused confession, absolution and Christian
burial until they had made restitution of their ill-gotten gains, and
any will they might make was invalid. All rulers and magistrates

23

of states or communities which permitted usury were themselves to be excommunicated.

In this atmosphere of hostility and prohibition, moneylending and pawnbroking were carried on in Britain, as in the rest of Europe, for nearly six hundred years. The groups mainly involved were the Jews; the 'Lombards', Italian financiers from the Medici states; and the Cahorsins, who derived their name from the French town of Cahors, in Languedoc, which was a famous centre of Italian financiers and money-changers in the Middle Ages.

The history of the Jews in England in the Middle Ages could hardly be described as happy. They were encouraged to settle here by William the Conqueror, and they remained for more than two hundred years until, in 1290, Edward I issued a proclamation ordering all Jews to leave the country. Such a drastic step was possible for two reasons. The Pope's strong condemnation of usury at the Council of Lyon sixteen years earlier had stirred up public hatred against the Jews, who had become the arch moneylenders, a detested symbol of an officially detested trade. And since by the end of the thirteenth century the 'Lombards' were in a position, whether banned by the Church or not, to meet all the royal borrowing requirements, the Jews were no longer indispensable, and Edward I, an incorrigibly spendthrift ruler, found it possible to dispense with their services without doing himself or his kingdom any great harm. He was, it has been nicely said, 'able to serve God without upsetting Mammon'.[7]

Having been ejected from England by Edward I, the Jews were not legally permitted to return for another three hundred and fifty years, although a few undoubtedly took up residence considerably earlier. Their remarkable ability to survive persecution and somehow make a living is an interesting part of medieval history. Mainly because of pressure from the Church, they were not allowed to be members of the guilds or to practise handicrafts. They had been increasingly forced out of agriculture and in country after country the development of a native merchant class made it difficult for them to engage in trade. There was consequently only a very restricted range of occupations which they could take up. Moneylending was one.

They were not subject to the canonical ban on usury, since their souls were considered to be irrevocably lost, and from the eleventh century onwards they turned their attention to finance. By the twelfth century Jew and usurer had become almost synonymous in many parts of Europe. Jews were, indeed, often permitted to settle only if they formally agreed to make loans. Provided sufficiently good security were offered, it was politically dangerous for a Jew to refuse to lend money.

But even with the help of the strong international and family links which existed within the Jewish community, the total amount of capital at the disposal of the Jews was relatively small, mainly because it was constantly being eaten away by mob attacks on Jewish people – there were particularly dreadful massacres following the coronation of Richard Coeur de Lion in 1189 – and by the special forced taxation which was imposed on the Jews from time to time. This persecution had one particularly important consequence so far as pawnbroking was concerned. During the twelfth century the Jews lent mainly to influential people, but by the thirteenth the Italians, with greater and more secure funds at their disposal, had captured the major part of this more prestigious and more lucrative end of the trade. The Jews by that time were confined almost entirely to lending to small borrowers, who could pledge only household and personal items. And it is precisely for this kind of pawnbroking that the evidence is so scanty: the borrowing habits of princes are much better documented. Certain facts are, however, available. One Jewish pawnbroker in London was sued for the return of a psalter, a medical book and a saddle, while the royal household accounts mention furs, silks and even cushions left as security with Jewish pawnbrokers, as well as the more normal pledges of jewellery and manuscripts.[8]

The situation was ironical. Because of the extremely precarious nature of their business, and to protect themselves, the Jews were compelled to charge high, sometimes very high, rates of interest. This in turn caused them to be condemned as extortioners and made them even more liable to attack and persecution. Whatever he did, the Jew could not win.

The Christians, mainly the 'Lombards' and Cahorsins, were more favourably placed than the Jews, although throughout the Middle Ages they had to contend with the disapproval of the Church, which was often considerably more than a formality. The Italian city republics were ahead of the rest of Europe in developing an economy which made it possible to separate trade and finance, and for the financiers to concentrate their activities and their capital entirely on making profits from lending money. Their resources and their reputation gave them a special standing in the other countries of Europe.

But, however much those in high places might need their services and protect them, they were never really secure. Edward III's failure to meet his obligations ruined two of the leading Florentine finance houses. The Cahorsins, whom Dante labelled as doomed to remain for ever in Hell, were expelled from England by Henry III in 1240, allowed back as a result of the direct intervention of the Pope on their behalf, but persecuted and imprisoned again in the following year, 'on account of their unbounded and detestable usury'. It was a dangerous calling, but apparently worth the risks involved, because by the end of the fourteenth century a network of pledging establishments had been created throughout Europe, concentrating on the top, and more profitable, end of the trade.

One of the pawnbrokers' principal customers during the later years of the thirteenth century was Guy, Count of Flanders, who held the title from 1278 to 1300. His financial resources did not match his ambitions, and he borrowed money on a scale that was enormous for the time. During the period of his rule there were Lombard pawnshops in several cities in the Netherlands, Bruges being the most important, and in one year the Count owed them a total of at least 6,800 lire,[9] or something like five million pounds in modern English money.

Charles the Bold, Duke of Burgundy, was a ruler who spent money equally freely. He had his own methods of compelling the pawnbrokers to meet his needs:

> In July 1473 the Duke suddenly revoked all the special licences to Lombard pawnbrokers throughout the Netherlands and seized their establishments. The sole purpose of the operation was to force the Lombards to advance a large loan, 14,000 écus, lent by the holders of 45 pawnshops, whereupon they were all allowed to resume business.[10]

Kings and princes not infrequently pledged their crowns. Sometimes the crowns were partly taken to pieces, so that individual jewels could be pawned separately. In 1340 five of the crowns belonging to Edward III and his queen were distributed in this way between two cities – Bruges and Antwerp – in the Netherlands, and two – Trier and Cologne – in Germany. A similar use was often made of religious ornaments and relics. It was partly for this reason that medieval rulers paid much attention to building up collections of jewellery; they needed to have valuable objects in hand to pawn as and when the occasion arose.

It was by no means uncommon for kings to use their nobles and leading churchmen as security. Edward III did this in 1340-1, when he sent the Earls of Derby and Northampton out of England to spend several months confined in Malines and Louvain respectively, as pledges for his debts.

In any age, pawnbrokers can carry on their business only if there are customers with suitable possessions to pledge, and as late as the seventeenth century most people had very few possessions. The homes of even comparatively prosperous people were, by modern standards, extremely sparsely furnished, and by no means everything they contained would have been of interest to a pawnbroker. Items of furniture were rarely acceptable as pledges; there was the problem, not inconsiderable under medieval conditions, of moving and storing it, and the danger of its destruction by fire, as well as the problem of finding a market for it if the pledge was not redeemed. Then as now, the pawnbroker preferred goods of high value and small bulk and, in terms of the thirteenth and fourteenth centuries, this meant mainly jewellery, gold and silver ware, pewter, saddlery, manuscripts and the more expensive kinds of textiles and furs.

In retrospect, the two most significant aspects of pawnbroking before the seventeenth century were its association with unchristian, immoral, anti-social practices and the gradual development of legal regulations to protect both the borrower and the lender. The first of these has lingered on into our own times – social attitudes and prejudices, once established, are very hard to change – and the second provided the basis of the code of practice which pawnbrokers came to follow during the nineteenth and twentieth centuries.

Throughout Europe by the fourteenth century pawnbroking, like other forms of lending, was controlled by special charters which defined the legal status of the lender, and laid down the limits of his responsibility for looking after the pledges entrusted to him, the conditions under which pledges could be forfeited and, sometimes but not always, the proportion of the value of the goods which might be given as a loan. Certain kinds of objects, such as

27

unfinished goods on which craftsmen were still working, could not be pledged at all. As early as the thirteenth century, charters specifying maximum interest rates were common. The figure most frequently found was 43⅓ per cent a year – twopence in the pound – but double this, 86⅔ per cent was not unusual. Broadly speaking, the further east one went, the higher the rates were likely to be, and everywhere during the Middle Ages it was normal to make 'foreigners', people not resident in the district, pay more.

During the second half of the fifteenth century, a number of charitable pawnshops, the *montes pietatis*, was established in central and northern Italy, in order to provide credit at low interest rates for small artisans and tradesmen and for the poorer classes in general. The first of these public pawnshops were started by a progressive Franciscan order known as the Observant Friars, who promoted them energetically and raised capital for them from municipal grants and private donations, topped up from time to time by such devices as church taxes and collections, a tax on legacies and the sale of indulgences. The interest rates were usually from four to twelve per cent but some small loans carried no interest at all. The maximum period of a loan was six to twelve months and any pledges which were not redeemed were sold at public auction, the borrower receiving any balance due to him after charges had been met.

The Italian *montes pietatis* were imitated, in a modified form, and on a smaller scale, in other countries, especially Germany, France and Belgium. The only European country which never went in seriously for this form of public enterprise was Britain, although even here there were some interesting eighteenth-century experiments, which will be described in the next chapter.

Somewhat curiously, the importance of pawnshops appears to have suffered a marked decline during the fifteenth and early sixteenth centuries. There are a number of possible reasons for this. The high rate of interest charged by the pawnshops had certainly given them a bad name. Interest charges were even higher than they might otherwise have been as a result of the widespread European depression during the fifteenth and early sixteenth centuries, which made it difficult to sell off pledges and added to the pawnbroker's risks. Whatever may have been the case among the better-off sections of society, ordinary people, who were particularly oppressed by the high interest rates, detested pawnshops.

During the fifteenth century, official measures were taken in many European cities and towns to force these rates down and to control the activities of pawnbrokers in other ways. In some places, private pawnshops were abolished altogether.

In Britain, there are reliable references to pawnshops by the end of the sixteenth century. One is known to have existed at Berwick in 1598 and another at Stony Stratford in 1624. The trade was certainly fairly carefully regulated at this time. Municipalities were in the habit of prohibiting all pawning except by officially recognised brokers who were required to be of good character and to keep a record of their transactions.

So far as Britain is concerned, the literary references to pawnshops and pawnbroking are extremely few before the end of the eighteenth century. There is virtually nothing in Shakespeare's plays – Shakespeare, oddly enough, does not seem to have been very interested in money – but one little scene in Ben Jonson's *Every Man in His Humour* (1598) provides some interesting sidelights on the nature and methods of the trade at that time.

Two men-about-town, Matheo and Bobadilla, are seeking a warrant for the arrest of someone who has attacked and affronted them. For this, however, they have to pay money to a third party, Musco, who demands five crowns for his services. Even between them, the pair are unable to raise such a sum, and the following dialogue takes place:

Matheo: Let's give him some pawn.
Bobadilla: Pawn? We have none to the value of his demand.
Matheo: Oh Lord, man, I'll pawn this jewel in my ear and you may pawn your silk stockings, and pull up your boots. They will ne'er be missed.[11]

Musco is not a pawnbroker, and the deal is subject to no kind of formalities. He may keep the pledges honestly and in safety, but, equally likely, he may appropriate them as a gift and either sell or pawn them quickly. But in any case they are easy to carry about and to store, and they are not difficult to dispose of reasonably profitably. 'Pawn' may not, in fact, mean quite what we may take it to mean. As Matheo and Bobadilla use the word it may signify 'goods instead of money' and 'pay in goods, not money'. It is this kind of complication which makes research into the history of pawnbroking so full of pitfalls and misunderstandings. Between the late sixteenth century and the late twentieth, key words can change their meaning in disconcertingly subtle ways.

Some of the words we take for granted are not as old as we might think. On the authority of the *Oxford English Dictionary*, the first recorded use of 'pawn', as a noun, in the sense of 'a pledge', can be dated 1496; the verb 'to pledge' is much later, 1570, and 'pawnbroker' even later than that, 1637. 'How,' one may well ask, 'did they pawn things without having the words with which to describe what they were doing?' The problem is not as serious as might be supposed. One can perfectly well take jewellery to a shop and borrow money on it without needing to have a special name for the man in charge, or for the activity with which one is concerned.

It is simply not possible to know what words people used when they visited a pawnbroker in 1600 or 1800. It seems very probable that at any date different social classes would have made use of different expressions, but one cannot be sure where the dividing lines would have been drawn. Consider, for example, the charmingly refined phrase, 'to lay or lay up in lavender', meaning 'to pawn', which is known to have been in existence in the 1590s and to have been favoured by the upper classes of society. Is this what Pepys's Lady Peterborough would have said in 1667, in an incident to which the diarist makes a sympathetic reference?

> The woman is a very wise woman, and is very plain in telling me how her plate and jewels are at pawn for money, and how they are forced to live beyond their estate, and to get nothing by his being a courtier. The lady I pity, and her family.[12]

Pepys was almost certainly sympathising with Lady Peterborough for the family's poverty, not for its connections with the pawnbroker, but in what words was she 'very plain in telling me' about her predicament? Did she say, 'We've had to lay our plate and jewels in lavender' or use similarly euphemistic terms? Or was it, 'We've had to pawn our plate and jewels'? Or something altogether different?

The question is an important one, because history is made up of attitudes, as well as facts. Attitudes, indeed, are a special and in no way inferior kind of fact, and in order to understand the past it is just as necessary and valuable to know what different types of people thought about pawnshops or Cromwell or press-gangs as to have the historical facts about these things at one's disposal. But we should not delude ourselves. Until very recent times, within living memory, we know and can know extremely little about the feelings of ordinary people towards the events, personalities and processes which were around them in their own lifetime, simply because nobody bothered to discover and to write the information down. We may infer from such clues as we have that, for example, most English people in the thirteenth century feared and disliked the Jews, but we cannot be sure. No reporters with notebooks and tape-recorders were touring Britain asking, 'Have you ever visited a pawnshop?' If they had done this, we might well have found it necessary to change what has been said earlier in this chapter.

Generalisations are always dangerous, and historical generalisations perhaps the most dangerous of all. Yet it seems safe to say that during the first half of the seventeenth century the philosophy and motivation of English society were undergoing radical changes. The commercial classes were coming to the top, with their demand, voiced with increasing confidence, 'that business affairs should be left to be settled by business men, unhampered by the intrusions of an antiquated morality or by misconceived arguments of public policy'.[13] To work hard, to be enterprising and self-reliant, was to carry out God's will and to deserve the name of Christian. What had previously been sins and social vices now emerged as economic and moral virtues. The rich deserved to be rich, the poor deserved to be poor, and the way was clear for the great eighteenth-century changes which are brought together under the portmanteau title of the Industrial Revolution and which provided unprecedented opportunities for banking, credit-giving and lending of all kinds, including, by the kind of historical accident that nobody could have foreseen, pawnbroking. Pawnbroking on the grand scale, lending money to the masses, was a child of the Industrial Revolution.

Pawnbroking was and is essentially an urban phenomenon. As towns and villages grew into cities, first drawing in an industrial proletariat from the countryside and then breeding their own, pawnbroking kept pace.

In 1600 the population of England and Wales was about four million, four-fifths of whom lived in the rural areas. London had something approaching 200,000 inhabitants and York, Norwich and Bristol perhaps 20,000 each. The average population of the other main provincial towns would have been about 5,000. By the

31

mid-eighteenth century, with the steam, iron, coal and textile revolution beginning to gather pace, London is estimated to have had a million and a quarter people, Bristol 80,000, Norwich 50,000, Manchester 45,000 and Birmingham 30,000. Within another fifty years, the population of all these cities had more than doubled.

The mere numerical growth of these cities as a consequence of industrialisation is not the most significant feature of the change that was taking place. What mattered much more was the quality and character of people's lives. The person in a town of 10,000 inhabitants is still experiencing life on a small scale, with the countryside close at hand and with a feeling of space. Once the figure of 100,000 has been reached, there have been fundamental changes. Life has inevitably become more organised, more regimented, more anonymous and more dependent on that essentially impersonal commodity, money. To be without money in a small town is uncomfortable; in a city it is disastrous. And at that point pawnbroking really begins to come into its own.

It is doubtful if pawnbroking, as a separate, self-sufficient trade, existed until the reign of James II, that is, before the 1680s. The Lombards combined the businesses of goldsmith, pawnbroker and banker, and this probably remained the most frequent situation, at least at the top end of the trade, until well into the eighteenth century. Samuel Pepys's Lady Peterborough almost certainly patronised a pawnbroker of this type.

In the early years of the eighteenth century, however, many goldsmiths gave up pawnbroking, probably because they felt threatened by the foundation in 1707 of a very large pawnbroking establishment called The Charitable Corporation for Lending Money to the Industrious but Necessitous Poor, set up on the model of the Italian *montes pietatis* to defeat 'the extortionate and usurious Rates made by Pawnbrokers', which at that time ranged from thirty to as high as sixty per cent. It had a capital which amounted to £600,000 at its peak and, despite its name, it was actually chartered to lend money on the security of pledges not only to the poor but to persons in more affluent circumstances. The Corporation went out of business in 1731, after the Common Council of London had charged it with receiving stolen goods and with providing prospective bankrupts with an easy and convenient means of swindling their creditors.

But by that time pawnbroking in London was in a very thriving

1 'Gin Lane' by William Hogarth, 1751: the first known representation of a British pawnbroker's shop (*left*).

2 An East End pawnshop, as seen by *The Illustrated London News*, 1886.

3 Outside a pawn-office at Merthyr Tydfil, 1875.

condition. In 1750 it was reckoned that there were about 250 large shops, with a much greater number of smaller establishments. In 1745 a committee representing the larger and more reputable pawnbrokers introduced into Parliament a Bill to protect themselves against 'divers Persons of ill Fame and Repute, who live in Garrets, Cellars, and other obscure places, taking upon themselves the Names of Pawnbrokers'. These second-line pawnbrokers were accused of a number of misdemeanours, including charging sixpence in the pound per week, 130 per cent interest, substituting inferior articles for those pledged, and selling pledges within as short a period as three months.

The Bill, which anticipated the Pawnbrokers' Act of 1756, proposed the licensing of pawnbrokers and permission to charge twenty per cent, a fifth of which was to go to hospitals and workhouses. It was a symbol of the size and importance which the pawnbroking trade had reached by this time.

The mid-eighteenth century is a watershed in another way, too. It was then that the three balls, either golden or blue, became generally adopted by pawnbrokers as a sign of their trade. Before then, pawnbroking establishments were distinguished by a variety of signs, although the 'Three Blue Balls' or 'Three Blue Bowls' were much the most frequent. Blue was, in fact, a more fitting colour than gold, since the sign almost certainly comes from the three blue discs which appear on the lower part of the coat of arms of the Medicis, from whose territory the Lombard goldsmiths originally came.

Why blue should have yielded place to gold is uncertain. A cynical but quite reasonable suggestion is that the pawnbrokers went for the gold sign when they ceased to be goldsmiths, but yearned for the prestige of gold. But, pleasant as it is, the popular explanation of the sign is certainly wrong: the three balls do not mean that the chances are two to one against anything pawned ever being redeemed.

NOTES

1 e.g. in the *Encyclopaedia Britannica*, 1973.
2 Chapter 23, Verse 19.
3 Chapter 23, Verse 20.
4 Chapter 24, Verse 6.
5 Chapter 24, Verses 10 and 11.
6 *Religion and the Rise of Capitalism*, Pelican edition, 1938, p. 43.
7 L. F. Salzman, *English Life in the Middle Ages*, 1926, p. 246.
8 On this see C. Roth, *A History of the Jews in England*, 1941, and R. J. Mitchell and M. D. R. Leys, *A History of London Life*, 1958.
9 *Cambridge Economic History of Europe*, Vol. III, 1963, p. 495.
10 Ibid, p. 506.
11 Act 4, Scene 7.
12 Entry for 3 October 1667.
13 R. H. Tawney, op. cit., p. 214.

3

The Georgian and Early Victorian Pawnbrokers: Problems and Opportunities

The hundred years from 1750 to 1850 were the period in which
pawnbroking in the British Isles experienced its greatest growth
and in which the pattern of the trade became shaped into a form
which is still recognisable today. Four Acts of Parliament during
the second half of the eighteenth century began a process of regulating the activities of pawnbrokers which culminated in the more
comprehensive Act of 1872, within the framework of which business has been carried on ever since, and which is only now drawing
to an end with the coming into force of the new Consumer Credit
Act.

In 1756, pawnbroking was made an exception to the general
maximum interest law, in 1784 a further Act established a maximum interest rate for all loans larger than ten pounds, and in 1785
the very important step was taken of obliging pawnbrokers to
register. The more comprehensive Act of 1800 contained a number
of specific provisions which helped to clarify the legal situation,
and gave both the pawnbrokers and their customers a more easily
understandable basis for their transactions. Limits were fixed on
charges – twenty per cent for loans of two pounds or less, fifteen
per cent for loans of forty-two shillings to ten pounds, and a ticket
charge of a half-penny to fourpence for loans of five shillings and
over, in proportion to the amount of the loan. The Act also fixed
the contract to be used and the form of the register which had to
be kept by the lender, controlled the length of time after which
pledges became forfeited – a year – and said how they were to be
disposed of by the pawnbroker. Pawnbrokers had to pay for an
Excise licence, which amounted to an annual tax on their business.

In Ireland the situation was rather different, and it is worth spending a little time discussing it, because some serious faults in the Irish legislation show what the consequences might well have been in the rest of the British Isles, too, if the way had been left open to corruption on this disgraceful and, from the point of view of the reputation of the trade, disastrous scale.

Until the 1780s, a law against usury, passed during the reign of George III, made it difficult to carry on pawnbroking legally in Ireland. Under the terms of this Act it was unlawful, in all circumstances, to charge more than six per cent for lending money. This rate of interest made it uneconomic to make loans for the small sums which had become normal by that time.

The two Acts which were passed in 1786 and 1788 and which related only to Ireland attempted to deal with a situation which was regarded on all sides as unsatisfactory. Henceforth, no loan was to be for more than ten pounds; a graduated system of interest rates was introduced for loans of more than one shilling and eightpence; there was a levy of a penny on the duplicate; and the pawnbroker was to be fined for any goods damaged while in his possession. Each prospective pawnbroker had to deposit a personal security of three hundred pounds, with three supporting securities of a hundred pounds each. The procedure for forfeited pledges was clearly laid down for both the pawnbroker and the auctioneer who sold goods on his behalf. These provisions were generally accepted as sensible and practical but, curiously, the Act contained no safeguards against pawnbrokers taking in stolen goods, an omission which was to cause great difficulties during the following century and which did much to bring the trade in Ireland into disrepute.

There was another serious weakness in the 1786 Act. The pawnbroking trade was placed under the supervision of the Marshal of Dublin, the City's chief administrative officer. Every pawnbroker had to make a monthly return to the Marshal of the number of pledges involved. For registering these details, the Marshal took a fee of a shilling. The pawnbroker also had to obtain a certificate from his local Town Clerk when he lodged his securities and this, too, had to be delivered to the Marshal.

It was soon evident that the 1786 Act gave far too much power to the Marshal and that a great deal of corruption was certain to arise from this. In particular, the appointment of the Marshal as the sole auctioneer of forfeited pledges in Dublin made it impossible for him to regulate the trade in a fair and disinterested way. The temptation and the opportunity to feather his own nest were too great.

Amending legislation was introduced in 1788 in an attempt to deal with these and other abuses, which were all too obviously rampant in the trade, and which the previous Act had encouraged rather than checked. The auction system was restructured, so that Dublin was divided for this purpose between four auctioneers, each of whose territory corresponded to one of the Dublin police divisions. Two of the four auctioneers were appointed by the Lord Lieutenant and the other two were the Marshal and the Sword-bearer. In practice, the new arrangement was no more satisfactory than the first. All it achieved, in effect, was to introduce corruption of a different kind; in each of the police divisions, a close association grew up between the pawnbroker and the auctioneer, to the mutual benefit of both, but very much to the disadvantage of the pawnbrokers' customers; although after 1788 auctions had to be advertised and detailed records of sales kept.

The 1788 Act did, however, bring about one or two minor improvements. After the passing of the earlier Act, there was a considerable amount of illegal pawnbroking, with unregistered moneylenders carrying out the functions of pawnbrokers. The law was now tightened up in this respect, at least in theory. An attempt was made to confine the trade to more solid and respectable persons. Securities were trebled – the new total of £1,800 represented a very considerable sum for the late eighteenth century – and the police had to issue a certificate of good conduct before a pawn-broker's licence could be renewed.

Between 1788 and 1843 there were no serious amendments to the legislation which regulated the activities of pawnbrokers in Ireland. The law was widely and flagrantly disregarded and the number of pawnbrokers mushroomed. It was 'a gamble for high stakes. The price of failure was bankruptcy: the reward for success was riches. And there were more than enough success stories to attract new operators.'[1]

Anything like satisfactory evidence as to pawnbrokers' earnings is hard to come by so far as the first half of the nineteenth century is concerned, whether for Ireland or for the rest of the United Kingdom. In addition to the regular, licensed pawnbrokers, there were a great many illegal operators, and even the officially approved pawnbrokers undoubtedly disregarded the law from time to time, particularly in the matter of the prescribed rates of interest. It so happens, however, that an American scholar has carried out the kind of painstaking research into Irish pawnbroking in the middle part of the nineteenth century which has produced information not so far available for the rest of the United Kingdom. Some of the facts discovered by Dr Raymond may also apply to England, although this possibility should be explored with great caution, because there were a number of important differences between the economies and social habits of the two countries. It has been estimated by Dr Raymond[2] that between 1830 and 1840 each pawnbroker in Dublin made an average annual profit of at least £950 a year, a very comfortable income indeed for the time, and that during the following decade this figure at least doubled. This should be set against the average annual wage of a skilled trades-man in Dublin during that decade, a little more than sixty pounds. Scattered pieces of evidence for England suggest there is no reason to suppose that the amounts would have been much, if at all, lower on that side of the Irish Sea. Pawnbroking was, of course, and always has been a highly skilled business, but for those with the necessary aptitude and experience in the trade, the rewards, at least up to the outbreak of the First World War, were attractive, so attractive, indeed, that the opinion was not infrequently expressed that such handsome incomes must indicate that the people earn-ing them were not operating wholly in the public interest and that some considerable strengthening of legal controls might be desirable.

To this, the answer then is what it is now, first, that no law has ever been devised which cannot be circumvented by those who are prepared to take the risk of doing so, and, second, that the law is only good to the extent to which it can be applied and administered. Outside Ireland the laws which governed pawnbroking in Georgian and Victorian Britain were, broadly speaking, sensible. They enabled the police and the courts to deal fairly and effectively with abuses and infringements and in general they were obeyed by the pawnbrokers themselves, because it was in their best interests to do so. The laws which applied to Ireland were a differ-ent matter. They contained such serious loopholes that corrup-tion and defiance of the law became far too simple a matter. Even more important, perhaps, they gave British pawnbroking as a whole a bad name. Bad news, as we well know, travels fastest, and the public had no difficulty in believing that what went on in Ireland must also be typical of the rest of the United Kingdom.

One can see, with hindsight, the magnificent opportunities which the Irish Acts presented to those who were determined to defy them both in the spirit and the letter. The behaviour of one Marshal of Dublin in particular, John Judkin Butler, who held office in the 1820s and 1830s, was nothing short of scandalous. He never inspected the books of either the pawnbrokers or the auction-eers, never checked to see whether the pawnbrokers complied with the regulations governing the sales of forfeited pledges, never asked for returns from provincial pawnbrokers, provided a fee of five pounds was paid in advance. Auction sales were conducted in remote parts of Dublin and all valuable articles were sold at night. There were no catalogues and the sales were often not advertised at all. The pawnbrokers and their agents monopolised the auction rooms and, being unsupervised, charged their clients an extortion-ate rate of interest.

The inevitable result of half a century of greed and malpractice was that by the 1830s the relationship between the pawnbroker and the Irish working class was exceedingly bad. Some improvement was brought about by the new Pawnbrokers' Act of 1843, which halved the rate of interest on loans under four shillings, brought in stringent regulations for auctions, and exposed delinquent pawn-brokers to severe penalties.

It is perhaps worth emphasising that in Ireland, as in the United Kingdom as a whole, the great majority of the pawnbrokers were Christians. One cannot, as happened so often in the Middle Ages, put all the blame on the Jews. In Dublin, as elsewhere in Ireland, pawnbroking was an essentially Roman Catholic occupation. The Jews were hardly represented at all among the fifty or sixty pawn-brokers active in the city[3] during the middle years of the nineteenth century.

Ironically, the most interesting pawnbroking experiment to take place anywhere in the British Isles during the whole of the nine-teenth century was in Ireland – Matthew Barrington's Charitable Pawn Office in Limerick, established as a direct result of the chaos, lawlessness and corruption which characterised Irish pawnbroking at the time. If pawnbroking in England had been as disorganised and as extortionate as it was in Ireland in the early part of the

39

nineteenth century, it is quite probable that institutions of the Mont de Piété[4] type would have been found here, too.

Barrington's plan was to establish a Mont de Piété for the benefit of the hospital and infirmary in Limerick. His pamphlet, *An Address to the Inhabitants of Limerick*,[5] explained the reasons for the scheme. 'With regard to the British dominions,' he wrote, 'we shall find these are the only countries of Europe in which lending money on pledges is used for private advantage exclusively, and in which the profits are not applied to some charitable or public purpose, and although various efforts have been from time to time made by the legislature to regulate the rate of interest, still it is found impossible to prevent the most dreadful excess in the charges. I admit pawnbroking to be an evil, but knowing at the same time that it is one that cannot be avoided, I propose (what is the next best thing to its suppression) to apply the profits of the trade to charitable and useful purposes.'

As a contemporary review of Barrington's pamphlet pointed out, the main reason why there were no Monts de Piété in England was that the trade was immensely profitable. There would have been strong opposition to any form of competition which might have taken away substantial numbers of customers. For all the controls imposed, British law treated pawnbrokers with remarkable kindness. Interest was calculated by the month, but most pledges were redeemed within the week. People who did in fact take back their pledges the same week were paying at that time the equivalent of 650 per cent per annum. A hundred pounds lent in this way in individual amounts of a shilling – a perfectly normal loan to a working-class customer – would, at compound interest, have produced nearly £46,000 in a single year. It would have been very difficult to invest one's money more satisfactorily elsewhere and, against this background, Raymond's estimate of £950 as the average annual profit of an Irish pawnbroker seems very conservative.

The Limerick project was successful in its early years, but it failed to obtain government support or the necessary continuity of enthusiasm and good management, and it gradually faded away.

The British pawnbroking legislation of the nineteenth century represented an attempt to mitigate the harsher social consequences of the profound changes which were affecting the trade during this period – its transformation from a source of financial aid to small businesses and to a declining section of the nobility to the poor man's banker, to provide small loans which would help working-class people to meet their day-to-day needs. The pawnbroker's new customers consisted of people living in the larger industrial and commercial centres whose income was barely sufficient when things were going well, and disastrously insufficient when there was illness or unemployment in the family. In 1796 Patric Colquhoun observed in his *Treatise on Indigence*[6] that the habit of pawning was 'exceedingly widespread' among the London poor and that 'if these modes of raising money were not accessible or were suddenly taken away, thousands would unavoidably perish in the streets'.

With the lifestyle of many of the London poor, or at least of its breadwinners, he had no sympathy at all. They were able, he believed, to earn enough to keep them and their family all the week by doing three or four days' work. Most of the rest of their time they spent drinking and talking in the public house. If they ran out of money, as they often did, the pawnshop was always at hand. They would pawn the coal at night to take out the blanket and the blanket in the morning to take out the coal. It appeared not to concern them that a substantial part of their wages was drained away by this incessant paying of charges to the pawnbroker. But the situation, Colquhoun observed, was going from bad to worse. There were, he understood, 240 pawnbrokers in London and the number was rapidly increasing.

Colquhoun castigated the London working class for 'improvidence and the total want of frugal habits or forethought', phrases which he would almost certainly never have thought of applying to members of the middle class who used the services of a different kind of banker to finance their more elevated business transactions.

By the end of the eighteenth century there was no shortage of moralists and social reformers anxious to tell the British poor how foolish and against their own interests their visits to the pawnbroker were. An article in *The Times* in 1797[7] made the point very plainly. 'Certain it is,' declared the writer, 'that, in many instances, 1/6th, and in some cases 1/5th, and even as high as 1/4th, of the earnings of the more thoughtless and dissolute part of the poor is paid for temporary accommodations.'

A person who borrowed threepence at a pawnshop every week, 'a thing very common', would be paying in interest '850 per cent on the sum borrowed', an annual charge even worse than that reckoned by the reviewer in the *Dublin University Magazine* in 1839 and, seen in this way, certainly worthy of the adjective 'extortionate'.

'This explanation,' felt *The Times*, 'should be a warning to those who are so improvident as to pawn their Sunday cloaths every Monday morning, or 52 times a year, a custom which too frequently prevails, without reflecting that the interest paid to the Pawnbroker would probably purchase two or three coats, gowns, or silk cloaks, in the course of a year. It ought also to be a serious caution against insuring in the Lottery, which, sooner or later, proves the ruin and destruction of all who suffer themselves to be cheated and deluded by trying their luck, where the chances are thirty to one against them.'

The warning, however well-founded it may have been, was not likely, however, to have been of much benefit to the people to whom it referred, for the excellent reason that very few of them were likely to have been readers of *The Times*, or indeed of any newspaper at all.

Perhaps the most significant aspect of the article was that *The Times* found pawnbroking worthy of its attention. It had become newsworthy. Colquhoun, although theoretically addressing himself to what he felt entitled to call the improvident working class, was in fact doing no more than identifying himself with the increasingly affluent and numerous middle class, many of the members of which were, by this time, showing a strong sympathy with the view that poverty was the result of a defect of character, an attitude which had become almost normal and respectable fifty years later.

It would be quite unjust, however, to regard all the early Victorian readers of *The Times* as lacking a sense of humanity. A letter in the paper's correspondence columns in 1826 makes this clear and shows a certain amount of hostility towards pawnbrokers. It reads as follows:

Sir – One of your correspondents will probably inform me, if the law permits pawnbrokers to retain the articles pledged with them if not redeemed within a twelvemonth. My strong impression is, that it does not; and yet these '50 per cent usurers' constantly refuse the redemption of goods after the stated period and the universal opinion among the poorer classes is that they can legally do so. I am led to make these observations from the effects of this belief in two recent instances, where a man with a large family, being reduced by a long course of sickness to extreme distress, was obliged to part with all his furniture, bit by bit, to keep his family from starving; and at the end of a year, being told by everyone that the pawnbroker's tickets were useless, he burnt them. Such, I have reason to believe, is the general impression throughout the metropolis; and, if an erroneous one, it cannot be too soon rectified. In these times of distress, there could not be a greater act of humanity than to inform the lower orders, by bills posted at different places, of the exact state of the law between the pawnbroker and the person pledging. And this might be done by any benevolent individual at very little trouble and expense.

A Constant Reader.[8]

An authoritative, although not very gracious or good-natured reply appeared in the next day's issue.

Sir – A question is asked in this morning's *Times*, 'if the law permits pawnbrokers to retain the articles pledged with them if not redeemed within a twelvemonth'. I have no time to waste, but I will answer this question, it being one that solely affects the distressed. The law does not permit pawnbrokers to retain articles pledged for more than 10s., if not redeemed within a twelvemonth, exclusive of the day of pledging; after the expiration of twelvemonths they are at liberty to sell, but are bound, if the property is not sold, to return it, and if sold, to pay the overplus to the owner. It is generally believed by the poor that the property pledged, if not redeemed within a twelvemonth, is not only forfeited, but that they have no claim whatever on the pawnbroker, either for the article or if sold, for the overplus. The case of Walter v Smith, 24 January 1822, which was fully stated in your journal of the day, decides the question. It is reported in Barnewall and Anderson's Reports, page 439.

I am, Sir, your obedient servant.   H.[9]

By the 1830s, pawnbroking had become of sufficient social and economic importance to attract the attention of the British Association for the Advancement of Science. The members of its Statistical Section had been looking for 'the best means of obtaining facts illustrative of the moral condition of the poorest classes of society'. The problem was admitted to be a difficult one, since morality does not easily lend itself to statistical treatment, but it was eventually decided that 'an accurate return of the number and nature of articles pledged in pawnbrokers' shops would throw great light on the subject'.

A large pawnbroker's shop in Glasgow allowed a Dr Cleland of that city to investigate and classify the pledges they had in stock on one particular day. The list furnished by Dr Cleland to the British Association's Annual Meeting in Bristol in 1836 was as follows:

539 men's coats; 355 vests;[10] 288 pairs of trowsers; 84 pairs of stockings; 1980 women's gowns; 540 petticoats; 132 wrappers;[11] 123 duffles;[12] 90 pelisses;[13] 240 silk handkerchiefs; 294 shirts and shifts; 60 hats; 84 bed ticks;[14] 108 pillows; 206 pairs of blankets; 300 pairs of sheets; 162 bedcovers; 36 table-cloths; 48 umbrellas; 102 Bibles; 204 watches; 216 rings; 48 Waterloo medals.

On the evidence of this small survey, the people of Glasgow appeared to be pawning the necessities of life, not luxuries. It was pointed out, however, that a detailed and accurate picture of pawning transactions in Britain was not possible, 'owing to the habits of the people of this country and the popular dislike of too minute an investigation into private affairs'. In France, however, where pawnshops were run by the Government, the task of collecting information relating to pawnbroking was much easier, and the British Association had made use of the statistical tables published annually by the French Ministry of Commerce in order to make certain deductions concerning the trade in Britain.

Putting the value of the articles into present-day British money, the average value of an article pledged in Paris in 1833 was 14.55 pence, but rather less in the provinces, being, for some unexplained reason, particularly low in Strasbourg. In the manufacturing towns, the number of pledges per thousand of the population tended to be rather higher than the average. Taking one town with another, between a quarter and a fifth of all pledges could not be redeemed by the end of the year, and one in twenty of all items pledged never returned to their former owners.

Assuming, as seems reasonable, that the situation in Britain was much the same as in France, the British Association's Statistical Section suggested that, after adjusting the figures to take the difference in population between Paris and London into account, about two million pledges a year were being made in London at that time and that the sum advanced on them exceeded one and a half million pounds. Since a very high proportion of the articles pledged were of small value and were repeatedly taken out and brought back by regular customers, the profits of a large, well-run business could be very great. Over and over again during the Victorian period we find people who would nowadays be called do-gooders castigating the poor for fecklessly pouring their pennies into the pockets of the pawnbroker. Here is a typical piece, from an 1836 issue of *The Penny Magazine*.[15]

The practice is most ruinous, and is the dearest of all possible means of obtaining money. It is lamentable to think that a sum, amounting every year to probably nearly £750,000 sterling, should be sacrificed in the greatest number of cases to provide the means of some momentary and unprofitable gratification, or, at best, to meet the exigencies which a little foresight and management would have prevented. Undoubtedly, there are cases in which these establishments silently furnish the means of relief to the truly unfortunate, in a manner probably less distressing than other modes; but the practice, when once it becomes habitual, is most pernicious. The facility of pledging the most trifling articles is attended with many evils, but it is difficult to perceive that they would be obviated by any direct impediment thrown in the way of such transactions. Any demoralisation which arises from the facilities afforded by respectable and authorised establishments can only be corrected in an indirect manner, by enlightening the people concerning their true interests, and by endeavours to elevate their moral notions.

From the point of view of the prudent, saving middle classes, this may well have been true, but the people directly concerned, the perpetually hard-up bottom layer of the urban pupulation, saw life quite differently. Then, as now, a high proportion of working-

45

class people lived only for the present. They existed and planned only from week to week. Whether this was from choice or from necessity is immaterial; it was their style and it reflected a philosophy fundamentally different from that of those who were always trying to convince them of the error of their ways. A modern comparison might be with industrial workers who lose their jobs and devote their redundancy money, not to building up a cushion against hard times, but to taking their family to Majorca for a couple of weeks or to buying a new car. Faced with the choice of immediate satisfactions or future benefits, a large number, possibly the majority, of our fellow citizens would always opt for immediate satisfactions or, as *The Penny Magazine* put it, 'momentary and unprofitable gratification'. There is a certain logic and common sense about this: tomorrow may never come.

The pawnbroker provided the means by which one survived another week, and possibly had a little pleasure in the process, and as long as there were a great many families living very close to the margin, he performed a useful and indeed an essential function. It is no exaggeration at all to say that he was an integral part of the Industrial Revolution and of the growth of British industrial power. The Victorian manufacturer prospered by paying his workers low wages; the pawnbroker and the high birthrate made it possible for him to go on doing so. If wages had been increased to a fair level, the pawnbroker would have become largely unnecessary, but to hire one's workers for a pittance and to offer them no security of employment and then condemn them for borrowing money to make ends meet was Victorian hypocrisy at its worst.

It may be helpful to draw attention to one aspect of the situation that is usually overlooked, that the People's Banking Service was provided by remarkably few people. In the 1830s there were 1,537 licensed pawnbrokers in Great Britain. Of these, 380 were in London and 61 in Scotland. Fewer than half employed a male assistant over twenty years of age; the remainder made do with one or two boys, together, of course, with the pawnbroker himself. The total number of people employed in pawnbroking in one capacity or another throughout the country would therefore not have greatly exceeded 5,000. According to the British Association's calculations, they would have handled a total of between five and six million pledges a year, most of them twice, once in, once out. Each pledge might well have required the services of three people, one to value it, one to make out the ticket, and one to put it away in the store. And this process, too, would have to be repeated in reverse when the pledge was redeemed. Critics of the trade might say that it was parasitical, extortionate and immoral, but they could hardly say that the people employed in it were not hardworking.

By no means all the pawnbrokers were men, although a study of local directories suggests that most of the women holding licences had taken over the business on the death of a husband or father. The *Bath Directory*, for example, lists seven pawnbrokers for the city in 1791. Two of these were women, but, as earlier directories show, both had succeeded their husbands.

It is often not easy to interpret the evidence provided by direc-tories. If a particular pawnbroker appears one year, but has dis-appeared the next, this may be because he has gone bankrupt, but it may equally well indicate that he has died or made enough money to retire or to set up in some other kind of business. Dr Raymond has noted[16] the high turnover of pawnbrokers in Dublin during the middle years of the nineteenth century – in 1865 more than three-quarters of the city's pawnbrokers had been in business for less than ten years – and much the same is true of the larger British cities.

Financial success, not surprisingly, brought a rise in social status. During the second half of the century, more and more pawn-brokers moved out of the back streets and into the better areas of town. When they started to become town councillors and Justices of the Peace, a development which will be discussed in the next chapter, their transformation from shady characters into pillars of the community was almost complete.

But as the prosperity of pawnbrokers increased, so did the attempts to defraud them. From the 1820s onwards *The Times* contains an increasing number of reports of such cases, and in the 1840s it was joined by *The Illustrated London News* which had a keen eye for this type of item. The three reports which follow illustrate the trend, and show the dangers to which pawnbrokers were exposed, and which made it necessary for them to charge a rate of interest which the public might consider high, but which to those in the trade was no more than the circumstances demanded.

In 1826 *The Times* carried a story of a kind which was repeated many times in subsequent years, about the manufacture of goods made specially to defraud pawnbrokers.

An entirely new imposition as to watches, which should operate as a caution to pawnbrokers in particular, and to the public in general, was attempted at the shop of Mr Morritt, in York-street, Westminster, on Friday last. Between the hours of seven and eight in the evening of that day, some person, who gave his name as William Smith, and who stated that he lived in Felix-street, Lambeth, offered a watch, pretending to be silver, to pledge, and requesting to be lent £1 upon it; when the shopman, Charles Johnson, asked Smith whether he would not be satisfied with 15s. on the article; the fact being that Johnson was suspicious of what is called the 'hallmark' stamped on the inside of the watchcase, and therefore he proposed to send a boy in company with Smith to his residence to inquire if it was all right before he advanced the 15s. to him. Leaving the watch in question in Johnson's hands, Smith went away with the boy; but when they got to Palace-yard, Smith was accosted by one of his associates, who inquired why he had been so long away. Here the confederates in depredation got rid of Morritt's boy, who returned home. Upon the examination of the proffered watch, it proved to be cased with very fine Britannia metal, neatly edged, and looking like silver by candle-light. The dial-face was handsome, the movement had the semblance of being sound, and the whole machine was certainly got up in a superior style. Numbers of similar watches are already prepared for circulation.[17]

The Times, like *The Illustrated London News*, was written and published for the middle and upper classes. The editors included the kind of news which, in their experience, was likely to be important to such people and to interest them. What was offered included a careful selection of crime, presented in a straightforward manner, so as to avoid the slightest accusation of sensationalism. The stories about pawnbroking which occur in their pages from time to time are nearly always concerned with some kind of fraud involving valuables, presumably since it was this aspect of a pawnbroker's business which was thought most likely to affect well-to-do people. The run-of-the-mill side of the trade – clothing and domestic goods – was not felt appropriate to the propertied classes or to the level of journalism which catered for them.

In consequence, an anthology of pawnbroking stories drawn

from these two publications, although fascinating in itself, would give an absurdly false idea of the trade as it was in Victorian and Edwardian times. What it would show, however, is the extent to which pawnbrokers found themselves involved, usually much against their will, with criminals and therefore with the police. There is a widespread popular belief that pawnbrokers have always been the nation's receivers of stolen goods *par excellence*, a welcoming haven for thieves, burglars and tricksters.[18]

This myth will be discussed at some length in later pages, but meanwhile one can simply say that the pawnbroker who receives stolen goods, knowingly or unknowingly, is and always has been in a most dangerous situation. If he accepts pledges, knowing them to have been stolen, he becomes an accessory to the crime, and liable to face prosecution on a criminal charge. Should he be convicted, he will certainly lose his licence and consequently his means of livelihood. If, on the other hand, he takes them in good faith, he runs the risk of losing the amount he has advanced on them, together with the goods themselves, once the true owner has satisfied a court of his right to repossession. In practice, pawnbrokers as a class have taken great pains to keep on good terms with the police, often at considerable inconvenience and expense to themselves.

A report published in *The Illustrated London News* in 1844, under the heading *Lady Shoplifters*, describes a situation which most pawnbrokers would have given a great deal to avoid.

On Saturday afternoon, about five o'clock, two elegantly-dressed women entered the shop of Mrs Rose, jeweller, etc., Farringdon-street, and, after looking at several articles, made a small purchase, and departed. Mrs Rose, however, having had reason to suspect them, sent her lad to watch them, and, after proceeding down Farringdon-street, the younger person entered the shop of Mr Flemming, pawnbroker. As soon as she had left the shop, the boy entered, when he found that she had pledged a handsome gold locket for £2. The lad now followed them and gave them into the custody of police-constable Adams, 214, who conveyed them to the Fleet-street police-station, where the younger woman was perceived to drop a knife from a pocket made in her boa. The knife, which was a silver one, was identified by Mrs Rose as her property, and the locket above alluded to was subsequently identified as the property of a silversmith in Cheapside. The women gave their addresses, Mrs Enshaw and Miss Wells, No. 5 Park-street, Camden-town, where City police-constable Wardle, 325, accompanied by the above constable, was sent, and on arriving at their apartments the constables found clothing of the most costly description, all of which, together with seven trunks and one carpet bag, were removed in a coach to the Fleet-street police-station, where the boxes and carpet-bag, on being opened, were found to be literally crammed with silks and satins, etc., chiefly not made up. In one of the trunks was found a quantity of jewellery, consisting of gold watches, brooches, rings, etc. One of the watches is stated to be worth £30. This trunk contained also 25 sovereigns. The whole of the property found is estimated at between £300 and £400.[19]

Mrs Enshaw and Miss Wells were, of course, professional thieves. John Parry, who was operating in Liverpool in the same year, was something more, a person whose working tools consisted of articles made specially in order to deceive and defraud pawnbrokers.

On Tuesday last, a middle-aged man, dressed in a suit of shabby-genteel black, named John Parry, was brought before Mr Rushton, at the Police-court, on a charge of having obtained money to a considerable extent upon false pretences, under the following circumstances – Mr Commissioner Dowling briefly stated the case, and said the prisoner had succeeded in obtaining money principally by pledging rings and crosses at pawnbrokers' establishments as gold, which were not gold, and in some instances selling the articles, which were most ingeniously wrought, and edged with gold, and the bulk of which was platina, mixed with gold. It would be proved distinctly that he stated them himself to be gold; that he said that his son brought them from Malta, and that they were composed of Maltese gold; and, under these circumstances, the charge would assume a felonious complexion and warrant the description applied to it, of obtaining money under false pretences. A number of pawnbrokers' clerks having deposed to the facts on oath, Mr Rushton said the articles were skilfully constructed, and that they were evidently made of platina, which was a heavy metal, and cased with gold – Mr Jones, Silversmith, of Castle Street, examined the rings and crosses, and said that the former were only lined with gold, and that the substance was silver or some other metal. The outside consisted of a thin coat of gold, and the value of each would probably be about 4s. or 5s. The crosses were of the same description of material, and the value of each would be about 3s. or 4s. The prisoner was committed for trial.[20]

To protect themselves against criminal activities and to press for government action in fields where their interests were threatened, pawnbrokers in different parts of the country began, from the 1830s onwards, to form local associations, which were also responsible for organising welfare schemes and social events. These corporate activities were a feature of the second half of the century, rather than the first, but it is pleasant to be able to end the present chapter with a reference to something other than crime.

On 22 June 1849, the Lord Mayor of London laid the foundation stone of the new almshouses provided by the Pawnbrokers' Charitable Institution, at Forest Gate, West Ham. With the stone safely laid, 'his Lordship partook of a collation provided by the Committee'. The London pawnbrokers could be said to have arrived. The Lord Mayor had set the seal of respectability upon them.

NOTES

1 Raymond James Raymond, 'Pawnbrokers and Pawnbroking in Dublin, 1830–1870', *Dublin Historical Record*, Vol. XXXII, No. 1, December 1978, p. 18.
2 Ibid, p. 18.
3 On this, see Louis Hymans, *The Jews of England*, 1972, pp. 133–60.
4 The French term became more commonly used than the earlier Latin form, *montes pietatis*.
5 Dated 18 December 1839. In the National Library of Ireland Pamphlet Collection, No. 76. It is discussed in an article, 'Pawnbroking in Ireland', *Dublin University Magazine*, Vol. XIV, 1839.
6 p. 237.
7 20 March.
8 27 January.
9 28 January.
10 i.e. waistcoats.
11 A woman's loose outer garment.
12 A thick flannel shawl or cloak.
13 A woman's long coat.
14 Linen cover of a mattress or featherbed.
15 29 October.
16 Op. cit., pp. 22–3.
17 26 February 1826.
18 See, for example, the image of the pawnbroker presented by Sir Arthur Conan Doyle in 'The Disappearance of Lady Frances Colefax', one of the stories in *His Last Bow* (1918). A quantity of jewellery belonging to Lady Colefax had been stolen by Dr Schlessinger, alias Holy Peters, 'one of the most unscrupulous rascals that Australia has ever evolved'. The whereabouts of both the criminal and the jewellery were a mystery, 'and then suddenly, after a week of helpless suspense, there came a flash of light. A silver-and-brilliant pendant of old Spanish design had been pawned at Bovington's, in Westminster Road.' Sherlock Holmes was jubilant. 'It is possible,' he said to Dr Watson, 'he will go to some other pawnbroker in the future. In that case, we must begin again. On the other hand, he has had a fair price and no questions asked, so if he is in need of ready money, he will probably come back to Bovington's.' The moral is clear: if you are looking for stolen goods, think first of the pawnbroker.
19 24 February 1844.
20 *The Times*, 25 May 1844.

4

From the Great Exhibition
to the Death of Queen Victoria

1851, the year of the Great Exhibition, was also the year of the Census. One part of the published report was headed 'The Occupations of the People in Great Britain and the Islands in the British Seas in 1851'. It revealed a grand total of 4,367 pawnbrokers of both sexes, or roughly one to every 7,200 of the population. The distribution was, of course, extremely uneven, with a heavy concentration in London, the manufacturing areas and the ports and relatively few pawnshops in the country districts. In some of the thickly populated urban areas there was one pawnshop to every 2,000 people.

It would be somewhat misleading to refer to any particular period as the golden age of pawnbroking, but the second half of the nineteenth century would have as good a claim as any to that title. It saw the passing of the Pawnbrokers' Act of 1872, which regulated the trade for more than a century; the establishment of the National Pawnbrokers' Association; and the considerable development of *The Pawnbrokers' Gazette* and an extension of its influence which, among its other useful features, provides the historian with a range and quality of information not previously available. Most important of all, this was the period in which a large number of what one might call the more solid pawnbroking concerns were established, the firms with stamina, family businesses founded by men who took an active part in public affairs and who helped to give the trade an altogether better image than it had had in its buccaneering days of fifty years earlier.

One saw this particularly well in Glasgow. The trade there had grown fast. In the twenty years from 1831 to 1851 the number of pawnbrokers in the city rose from nineteen to fifty, in the face of

53

considerable hostility. City councillors, lawyers and the chief constable were actively antagonistic and the first attempt, made in 1840, to form a Pawnbrokers' Society, failed. A new Pawnbrokers' Protection Society, 'to protect the members from the numerous frauds of designing individuals', was established in 1851. Its first chairman, William Cameron, was a most respectable man. He had wanted to become a minister of the Church of Scotland, but the early death of his parents prevented this. Needing to earn his living as soon as possible, he first became a schoolmaster and after some years of this set up as a pawnbroker in Glasgow, at a time when the trade was in a turbulent state. He remained in this occupation for thirty years, finally retiring in 1862. Another Glasgow pioneer, William Warrington, who died in 1870 at the age of 78, was described as 'a man of literary taste and musical ability, and a cherished guest'.[1] Another pawnbroker, Henry Hutchinson, died in 1910 at the ripe age of 92. His three sons became respectively a clergyman, a doctor and a lawyer.

An even more remarkable man was Watson Mackay, the Association's Secretary in 1859–60. 'He had studied medicine for a time and this led to him trying his hand at teeth extraction, an art in which he gained some mastery. He extracted teeth in his business premises, gratuitously, for any sufferer, old or young. It is related that the weavers, when hard up, were wont to feign toothache and have Mackay extract the tooth, on the chance that he would follow his usual custom and offer a glass of good Scotch whisky as solace. He also conducted a free school for young weavers, to whom he imparted knowledge from 9.30 till 11 in the evenings, after their long day at the looms was over. Later he retired from business and went to reside at Dunoon where he became Provost.'[2]

The Glasgow pawnbrokers took the most energetic measures to improve their reputation. These included employing women as spies to obtain evidence which might lead to the conviction of the proprietors of the so-called 'wee pawns', who paid little attention to the regulations of the Pawnbrokers' Act.

In England James Bowes of Manchester was an excellent example of the new breed of pawnbroker. He was the son of 'Honest John' Bowes, born in the year of Waterloo, a Chartist, President of the Manchester and Salford Co-operative Society, and 'a strenuous worker in many good causes throughout his long life'.[3] James Bowes was born in 1849, educated at Manchester Grammar

School, and served a seven-year apprenticeship in pattern-card making. Abandoning manufacturing industry, he entered the pawnbroking trade in 1875, working with his brother-in-law, Alderman Birkbeck. He set up on his own five years later. He was a Manchester city councillor for fifteen years and an alderman for ten, an active worker for the Liberal Party for forty years, a Justice of the Peace, Director of the Manchester Ship Canal, President of the Manchester Union Glee Club, and Junior Deacon in his masonic lodge. He became an international authority on trams, as a hardworking and successful Chairman of the Manchester Trams Committee.

In his retirement, a local newspaper paid tribute to him in these terms:

> Mr Bowes is an asset to any undertaking; he is sound and tactful and straightforward in his business methods, whilst socially he is a host in himself, 'hail fellow, well met', to a very large circle of friends, acquaintances and admirers . . . He is a fluent speaker, a zealous worker, and inspires confidence by his never-failing tact and courtesy . . . In his trading days and even now, he is heart and soul a Pawnbroker, but, there is no doubt about it, he is intensely happy in his public life, and he recommends it as a valuable opening for any man of leisure. His public work is watched by his colleagues in the Trade with the keenest interest, and, as we pointed out the other day, when he was selected for an introduction to his Majesty the King, the whole Trade rejoiced with him at the honour, which had its reflected glory on the Trade Alderman Bowes had long adorned.[4]

The firm of James Bowes Ltd is still in existence, under the control of the grandson of the founder, David Bowes. For most of the hundred years it has been trading, it combined pawnbroking with men's outfitting, soft furnishings and household ornaments.

One or two other businesses have their origins even further back than James Bowes Ltd. Mr Edwin T. Brown, now retired, recalls that his great-great-grandfather had a pawnbroking business in St Martin's Lane in the eighteenth century. In the later 1800s it was moved to Ryder's Court, Leicester Square, because the St Martin's Lane site was being redeveloped to build the London Coliseum. The Raselle pawnbroking business, in Old Market, Bristol, was established in 1793 and is still active on the same site. Another name well known in the trade for over a century is Thomson – not to be confused with Harvey & Thompson. Mr Douglas Thomson and his family at present control six pawnbroking businesses in the London area.

The name of Attenborough was well known among London pawnbrokers in the 1860s. Members of the family had businesses in various parts of London, mostly in the West End, and one or two of these still have pawnbroking departments, although in recent years jewellery has become the main interest. There were businesses under the name of Attenborough in Shaftesbury Avenue, Duke Street, Manchester Square and Fleet Street. Two branches of the family were solicitors and provided most of the legal services the trade required.

Fish Brothers Ltd, with six branches in London, have just celebrated their 150th anniversary and the present head of the firm, Mr P. W. Fish, has an interesting collection of documents relating to the activities of his predecessors. These include a letter applying for a position with Mr Fish's great-grandfather. It provides a number of interesting clues to the customs and state of the trade in the 1870s. Dated May 1875, it is written in a beautiful copperplate hand.

Sir,
   Wanting a re-engagement at the Counter (my present engagement terminating on the Twenty-seventh Instant) I take the liberty of writing to you to offer you my services, should you require them.

   I have been in my present situation seven years as Foreman residing on the premises with my Wife and family, my wife acting as Housekeeper.

   I am Forty-eight years of age and have had Thirty-five years' good practical experience in the Trade. My first situation was at Mr Reeves', Gray's Inn Lane, where I stayed Two years,
the next Mr Bayfield's, New Cut, Lambeth, Three years
then   Mr Ashford's, Bethnal Green Road, Five years
then   Mr Hawes', Whitechapel Road, Eight years
then   Messrs Dicker & Scarlett's, Commercial Road, Five
            years
and my present one at Mr Fileman's, Union Street, Seven years.

I am of steady and industrious habits, and work for others as I would do for myself. I take this way of making my wants known, as I do not want to be out of a situation with a Wife and three children dependent on me. Should you not require my services yourself, you might know some one who does.

I am,

    Yours respectfully,

    W. M. Fayerbrother

All Letters addressed to T. Maguire
          26 Garlick Hill, City.

Why, one wonders, was such an excellent man, 'of steady and industrious habits', so constantly on the move? Why should Mr Fileman have been willing to part with him? The probable answer is that, with a growing family, he was compelled to be always on the look-out for a situation which would pay him a few shillings a week more.

That pawnbrokers' assistants had to watch every penny of their income is shown by a set of accounts from Mr Charles Fish. These relate to a period five years after Queen Victoria's death, which is the appointed limit of the present chapter, but the position of the firm in 1906 is not likely to have been very different from what it had been five or even ten years earlier.

In 1906 Mr Fish held stock to the value of £6,544 1s. 1d. His outgoings, in the form of loans and purchases, amounted to £16,930 7s. 2d. and on this sum he made a gross profit of £1,421 12s. 2d. Against this, however, he had to set expenses of £805 12s. 8d., leaving him with a net profit of £616 os. 6d., which seems very modest indeed, in view of all the risks the business entailed.

The details of his expenses for the year are interesting:

	£	s.	d.
To rent	90	0	0
Rates and taxes (I. H. Duty)	35	7	9
Licences	13	10	3
Fire Insurance &c	14	13	6
Printing, Advertising, Stationery & Sundry Trade expenses	136	13	3
Repairs	21	4	9

	£	s.	d.
Electric Light & Gas	47	1	1
Salaries of Assistants	261	19	5
Housekeeping for do.	150	3	0
Bad debts	34	19	8
	805	12	8
Net Profit	616	0	6
	£1,421	13	2

We do not, unfortunately, have the details of the staff employed by the firm at this date, but a reasonable guess would be two men and two boys. The figure of £150 for 'housekeeping' suggests that three of them lived on the premises – £150 would hardly have been sufficient to lodge and feed more than this, even at 1906 prices, although with good management and a little parsimony four might just have been achieved.[5] The fourth person may well have been in the position of Mr Fayerbrother, with long experience of the trade and living on the premises with his family, his wife acting as housekeeper to a younger man and two boys. In such circumstances, 'housekeeping' in the accounts may have included some form of payment to the equivalent of Mrs Fayerbrother, or quite possibly the family received free accommodation in exchange for these services.

But, whatever hidden clues one may discover in Mr Fish's accounts – and factual information of this kind is extremely rare – it is clear that an honest, law-abiding, run-of-the-mill pawnbroker, which Mr Fish was, stood to make a comfortable living and no more. He was hardly on the road to wealth. It should be pointed out, however, that a pawnbroker's profit – Mr Charles Fish's £616 0s. 6d. – referred to the business as a whole, not to the pawnbroking part of it. Few reputable pawnbrokers would have found it possible to keep going at all without engaging in some form of retail trading, usually jewellery or outfitting, not infrequently both.

This point was made clear in the course of a correspondence in *The Times* during December 1870, when the ground was being cleared for the new Pawnbrokers' Act of 1872. *The Times* had published[6] a summary of the main points of the Report to a Select

Committee which had been doing its best to find out the facts about pawnbroking. The Report showed that on 31 March that year there were 2,476 registered pawnbrokers in the cities and boroughs of the United Kingdom – 1,735 in England, 378 in Ireland, 283 in Scotland, and 80 in Wales. In the counties, there were a further 793, giving a grand total for the whole country of 3,269 legally recognised establishments. *The Times* then went on to say that 'from statements handed in to the Committee from three pawnbroking establishments, the net earnings were shown to be respectively 10.271, 8.184 and 6.351 per cent on capital'.

This brought a prompt reply from Alfred Hardaker, a Liverpool pawnbroker, who was at that time the Honorary Secretary to the Pawnbroking Parliamentary Reform Association. 'Will you allow me to say,' he asked, 'that these results were not produced by the operations of pawnbroking only, but in combination with sale departments, in which new jewellery, clothing, etc. were largely dealt in? If you will kindly refer to section 3, in Statements A and B, you will find that the net earnings in the pawnbroking departments of those two businesses were 5.640 and 6.091 per cent on capital respectively. Your quotation in respect of the third business is correct, as no new sale stock was kept; consequently, the whole of the profits were derived from the pawnbroking business.'[7]

One of the main difficulties facing Mr Hardaker and his colleagues was that what one might call the non-pawning section of the British public – most of the middle and upper classes – appeared to make no clear distinction between the legal and the illegal, the licensed and unlicensed sections of the trade. The malpractices of the second were always being laid at the doors of the first, much to the annoyance of those who took pains to operate within the limits of the law.

The dolly-shops or, as the Scots called them, the 'wee pawns' or 'low brokers', were an unsavoury feature of Victorian life. The best description of them is to be found in Henry Mayhew's *London Labour and the London Poor*, which shocked middle-class Britain when it appeared in the 1860s.

Mayhew reported:

The dolly system is peculiar to the rag and bottle man, as well as to the marine-store dealer. The name is derived from the black wooden doll, in white apparel, which generally hangs dangling over the door of the marine-store shops, or of the 'rag-and-bottles', but more frequently the last-mentioned. This type of the business is sometimes swung above other doors by those who are not dolly-shop keepers. The dolly-shops are essentially pawnshops, and pawnshops for the very poorest. There are many articles which the regular pawnbrokers decline to accept as pledges. Among these things are blankets, rugs, clocks, flock-beds, common pictures, 'translated' boots, mended trowsers, kettles, saucepans, trays, &c. Such things are usually styled 'lumber'. A poor person driven to the necessity of raising a few pence, and unwilling to part finally with his lumber, goes to the dolly-man, and for the merest trifle advance, deposits one or other of the articles I have mentioned, or something similar. For an advance of 2d. or 3d., a halfpenny a week is charged, but the interest is the same if the pledge be redeemed the next day. If the interest be paid at the week's end, another 1d. is occasionally advanced, and no extra charge exacted for the interest. If the interest be not paid at the week or fortnight's end, the article is forfeited, and is sold at a large profit by the dolly-shop man. For 4d. or 6d. advanced, the weekly interest is 1d.; for 9d. it is 1½d.; for 1s. it is 2d., and 2d. on each 1s. up to 5s., beyond which sum the 'dolly' will rarely go; in fact, he will rarely advance as much. Two poor Irish flower girls, whom I saw in the course of my enquiry into that part of street traffic, had in the winter very often to pledge the rug under which they slept at a dolly-shop in the morning for 6d., in order to provide themselves with stock money to buy forced violets, and had to redeem it on their return in the evening, when they could, for 7d. Thus 6d. a week was sometimes paid for a daily advance of that sum. Some of these 'illicit' pawnbrokers even give tickets.[8]

The dolly-shops, as Mayhew pointed out, did an immense trade. They were notorious as receivers of stolen property, especially of clothing, a good deal of which was taken surreptitiously from the clothes-lines of the well-to-do. But there is, alas, no doubt that some licensed pawnbrokers also took in goods in the knowledge that they had been stolen, though many more were innocent victims of criminal activity and often suffered financially as a result. As a general rule, the more valuable stolen items were likely to find their way to a pawnbroker, while clothing and other pledges of relatively low value came into the hands of the proprietors of the dolly-shops. Servants were often the guilty parties. Mayhew shows us how and why this happened.

There are many felonies committed by the male servants in gentlemen's families; some of them of considerable value. Numbers of these are occasioned by betting on the part of the butlers, who have the charge of the plate. They go and bet on different horses, and pawn a certain quantity of plate which has not the crest of their employer on it, and expect to be able to redeem it as soon as they have got money when the horse has won. He may happen to lose. He bets again on some other horse he thinks will win – perhaps bets to a considerable amount, and thinks he will be able to redeem his loss; he again possibly loses his bet. His master is perhaps out of town, not having occasion to use the plate. On his return home there may be a dinner party, when the plate is called for. The butler absconds, and part of the plate is found to be missing. Information is given to the police; some pawnbroker may be so honourable as to admit the plate is in his possession. The servant is apprehended, convicted, and sentenced possibly to penal servitude. Cases of this kind occasionally occur, and are frequently caused by such betting transactions.[9]

'Some pawnbroker may be so honourable as to admit the plate is in his possession', the implication being that not all pawnbrokers would, in fact, have behaved in this exemplary fashion. A few years earlier there had been the case of Lady Honoria Cadogan's bracelet. Lord Cadogan, who had recently died, was a great collector. Many of the items in his collection had been left to various members of his family, and the remainder were to be sold. A man named John Wright was in the Cadogan family home for the purpose of making an inventory of the articles intended for disposal. While he was on the premises he stole a bracelet and other jewellery belonging to Lady Cadogan. The following day he sold the bracelet for ten guineas to Richard Attenborough, the Piccadilly jeweller and pawnbroker. Mr Attenborough, having seen a description of the missing bracelet, was able to help the police to arrest the thief, but Lady Cadogan never got her property back, because, immediately Attenborough's had bought the bracelet, the stones were taken out and disposed of to another pawnbroker for £18 and the gold went

61

to a man in Hoxton for melting down. Fortunately this happened over the Christmas period when little work was being done, and the bracelet, minus, of course, its stones, was recovered just before it disappeared for ever. The stones, however, were never seen again.

'The subject,' believed *The Times*, 'concerns every man who has a watch in his pocket or a basket of plate in his house, and every lady whose rings or other trinkets are of sufficient value to attract a thief.'[10] If the bracelet had been disposed of, 'not at a first-rate establishment in Piccadilly, but at the late Mr Fagin's, in the neighbourhood of Saffron Hill, there would be all sorts of ugly suspicions and a strong tendency to give a jury the duty of pronouncing on the conduct of both parties to the transaction'. Mr Attenborough, in other words, could have counted himself lucky not to have been in court on a charge of receiving stolen goods.

When it looked into the matter more closely, *The Times* was informed by one of Mr Attenborough's assistants that what had taken place was normal practice in the trade. Old-fashioned jewellery was nearly always broken up and sold off at once. It was, he said, 'a matter of principle'.

The Times then moved into the attack, without feeling the slightest need to mince its words:

> The principle in this case [it reminded its readers, and especially 'the more wealthy and tasteful people'], was to buy a bracelet of the reign of Charles II for ten guineas without examination or delay, and at the mere word of the seller, though it was so intrinsically valuable that the loose stones were sold that very day for £18. That such a peculiar piece of jewellery should be offered for sale at so low a price does not excite the smallest surprise in experienced pawnbrokers, who took it in the regular course of business; and when their conduct is questioned one of them makes a merit of having given any information at all on the subject. This may be quite regular, and the usual mode of doing business, but, so far as the public interests are concerned, we can see no difference between the practice and that of the persons who are proverbially said to be worse than thieves. In either case the man who sees a valuable article and is tempted by it equally knows that he has a ready means of turning it into money. He will not be obliged to send

the gems abroad, or to consort with disreputable receivers, for he can walk into a respectable establishment, and in a few minutes dispose of his spoil with a reasonable belief that the material evidence against him will be instantly destroyed. In fact, without imputing any dishonest intention to these trades-men, and fully believing that they follow only an evil tradition which teaches them that a too rigid examination of customers is bad for business, and that they have no need to meddle with what does not concern them, we must demand, in the name of the public, that they will reconsider their mode of doing busi-ness, and give fewer facilities for the sale of valuable property. It may certainly happen sometimes that a person pressed for money wants to part with a watch or a ring at once, but a little discrimination will easily enable the purchaser to judge whether he is dealing with a legitimate owner. In such a case as the present, however, there was real reason for caution. So respect-able a tradesman should have hesitated to deal with an unknown person who offered a piece of antique jewellery for little more than half the value of the stones. Such practices can have but one effect – to attempt to the commission of thefts, and unless they are abandoned the matter will require the serious con-sideration of those who enact and administer the law.

The case attracted considerable attention, and Mr Attenborough and his staff would certainly appear to have behaved with less wis-dom than one might have expected. The next day[11] – the prompt-ness is significant – someone signing himself 'A West End Jeweller and Pawnbroker' took up the challenge. It was not, he insisted, 'the custom of West End jewellers and pawnbrokers to buy expensive jewellery of strangers without enquiry', nor was it a matter of principle with them 'to break up old-fashioned things as soon as bought'. Mr Attenborough's assistant should not have tried to excuse his conduct in such a ridiculous fashion. His personal 'principles' should not be taken as being those of the trade as a whole.

In one way or another, Victorian pawnbrokers were rarely out of the news for long, which is an indication of the important place they occupied in the national life. They were most frequently mentioned in connection, not with any misdemeanour on their part but with frauds and trickery practised upon them. Some of these were exceedingly ingenious. Thomas Collins had pawned a portrait of Lord Desart, which he had obtained from his lordship by pretending he was preparing for publication a work to be called *Portraits of Eminent Conservatives*.[12] Other gentlemen, it appeared, had parted with their portraits for the same reason, and all the pictures had finished up in pawnshops. Louis Mouilliett had obtained thirty pounds on the security of two hogsheads of port wine, which later turned out to be 'an equivalent quantity of indifferent water'.[13] The pawnbroker had taken the precaution, as he thought, of tapping the hogsheads when they were first delivered to him, but what he was in fact tapping was only a very small container immediately behind the bung.

So far as one knows, Mr Mouilliett was not in the habit of pawning hogsheads of bogus port. News travels fast in the pawnbroking world and a trick of this kind could hardly have succeeded a second time. But other swindles were carried out on an industrial scale by professional criminals. One interesting technique came to light in 1885, when police investigations showed that a gang in London had been doing very well by making and pawning sovereigns and articles of jewellery of what was referred to as 'mystery gold', a composition of tin, platinum and copper which defied the usual acid test and weighed as much as pure gold.[14]

One man who tried to rob a pawnbroker came to a very unpleasant end. He belonged to a gang which had planned to break into a pawnbroker's establishment in Liverpool. His particular part in the enterprise was to enter the premises down the chimney, but he got stuck halfway and stayed uncomfortably fixed there with a fire burning below him. His groans and shouts attracted attention and a hole was made to release him, but he died from suffocation soon after his rescuers reached him.[15]

Sometimes the cases which interested the Press were merely bizarre, involving no criminal act at all. In 1864 a Mrs Till, who was of advanced years, asked Mr Elliott, the magistrate at Lambeth Police Court, for his advice and help.

She said that, on the 4th of April last, she pledged eight shillings at the shop of Mr Aymas, a pawnbroker in Lambeth-Walk, for sixpence, and, having since lost the ticket, she called there on that day to take the pledge out or receive an affidavit on it. – Mr Elliott: I cannot understand you. Do you mean to say that

4 Saturday night at a London pawnbroker's, 1906.

5 The furniture room in a London pawnbroker's warehouse, 1906.

6 A London pawnbroker's store, 1906 : storing bundles
in the weekly pledge room.

7 Burns's pawnshop, Millwood and Clayton Streets, Glasgow, 1926.

8 A sale of unredeemed goods at Debenham, Storr and Co.,
London, 1906.

9 Parker's, Middlewood Road, Sheffield, c. 1920.

you pledged eight shillings in silver for sixpence? – Applicant: Yes, your Worship. – Mr Elliott: What was your object in doing so extraordinary an act? – Applicant: The fact, your Worship, was that I was going into the workhouse, and, knowing that the money would be taken from me, I adopted that means of securing it. – Dixon, the usher, said that this was commonly done by persons going permanently into the workhouse. It was their practice at the workhouse, on persons going there to stop, to take off their clothes and wash them, and all the money found on them was appropriated to their support: and the sixpence which the applicant received she could keep in her mouth during the operation of washing and preserve it from her searchers.[16]

Pawnbrokers themselves appeared before the courts from time to time, charged with breaking the regulations which governed the trade, but, before giving one or two examples of these offences, one should perhaps point out that the courts have always been to pawnbrokers what the General Medical Council has been to doctors, the means of disciplining erring members of the profession. Just as the majority of doctors or lawyers never appear before a disciplinary tribunal in order that a charge of malpractice can be investigated, so very few pawnbrokers in any generation are prosecuted by the courts. Those who are inevitably make news. If doctors by the dozen were being struck off the register each year, or if a pawnbroker a week was going to prison, the incidents would very soon cease to be given space in the newspapers. The fact that such cases are considered worthy of being reported is a symptom of a healthy profession rather than the reverse.

The Victorians were able to bring pawnbrokers before the magistrates precisely because the law governing the trade was so strict. The charges brought against them were usually of one of three kinds – requiring more than the legal rate of interest; knowingly receiving stolen property; and accepting pledges from minors. In 1864, 'at the Clerkenwell Police Court, a pawnbroker has been fined 20s. and costs for charging more than the legal interest on certain articles pledged at his shop'.[17] In 1873, when a bootmaker was convicted at Worship Street Court of fraudulently pawning his employer's property, the magistrate condemned the conduct of the pawnbrokers as 'extremely reprehensible',[18] and at Hammersmith in the same year, Eliza Clayton was charged with stealing and pawning property worth £300 from her employer. She was sent for trial, leaving the judge to decide what should be done with the pawnbroker.[19]

These were not particularly remarkable cases, but occasionally one comes across one with original features to it, like the one heard at Thames Police Court in 1868, when a pawnbroker called Lowenburg was accused of several serious offences. A pawnbroker was permitted to charge a halfpenny for each ticket when the amount advanced was less than five shillings. Mr Lowenburg had discovered an ingenious method of doing better for himself:

> The accused, in order to increase his profits, was in the habit of dividing articles brought to him, so as to require more tickets for the pendulum and weights, and Mr Gowland (the prosecuting solicitor) said he could bring seventy cases forward of the same kind. The defendant was fined in all the charges brought against him, the aggregate, with costs, being £14 2s. It was stated on behalf of the Pawnbrokers' Protection Society that no such practice as that adopted by Lowenburg, of dividing a pawn or pledge, was known in the trade.[20]

From a pawnbroker's point of view, the most serious aspect of a conviction was not the fine, but the strong possibility that the police would oppose the renewal of his licence. Someone who had behaved as Mr Lowenburg had could hardly be described as a person of good character, which the law required a pawnbroker to be.

Pawnbrokers' assistants sometimes found themselves in trouble with the law. In 1871 Thomas Davis was committed for trial, charged with stealing a large quantity of jewellery from his employer, a Birmingham pawnbroker. Davis had evidently operated on the grand scale. A deficiency of £1,800 had been detected during stocktaking. Most of the stolen goods had disappeared, but when the assistant's house was searched jewellery to the value of nearly £300 was found in it, consisting mainly of gold and silver watches and chains, rings and brooches.[21] Two years later, two youths, 'respectably connected', were caught by a detective 'in the act of wholesale plunder from the warehouse of their employer, a pawnbroker'.[22]

From the 1870s onwards, one has a much better source of information about the trade, in the form of the greatly expanded and improved *Pawnbrokers' Gazette*. This published the less sensational kind of material, which rarely found its way into the columns of the ordinary press, and consequently allows one to build up a fuller and better balanced picture of the pawnbroker's life and work than was previously possible.

There are, for example, the advertisements of businesses for sale. These provide interesting sidelights on the character and attractions of the trade. For £1,600 one could buy 'an old-established Pawnbroking and Sale Business in the Country', complete with stock and house. There was 'no other pawnbroker within sixteen miles' and the location, not specified, was 'in the centre of a good agricultural district', presenting 'a rare opportunity for the safe investment of a small capital'.[23] Similarly recommended was 'a pawnbroking business in the main street of Batley, it being one of the most thriving towns in the West Riding of Yorkshire. Attached is a splendid sale shop, with double plate glass windows, where all the unredeemed goods might be sold, if properly looked after.' This, too, was felt to offer 'a first-class opening for a small capitalist'.[24]

The last point is important. Despite the myth of great wealth which surrounded it, pawnbroking in Victorian England was a trade one could enter with a very modest amount of capital and with the reasonable expectation of earning a respectable income within five or ten years, although a pawnbroker in Leeds is on record as having said that his trade brought a smaller return on capital than running a draper's or grocer's shop.[25] A high proportion of new pawnbrokers had gained the necessary experience as assistants and, after saving for twenty years or more, had managed to accumulate enough to acquire a business of their own. It was certainly not an occupation for amateurs or *dilettanti*. Too many unscrupulous people were lying in wait to cheat the pawnbroker at the first chance that presented itself.

One gets the impression that many, possibly most pawnbrokers would have made excellent detectives or customs officers. A pawnbroker in High Street, Whitechapel, for instance, was struck by the contrast between the appearance of Ann Greer, 'a dirty-looking woman', and the goods she was attempting to pledge with him, a set of gold false teeth worth £3 10s. He informed the police and the woman was arrested.[26] The assistant of Mr Charles Thompson, a Coventry pawnbroker, had an equally well-developed instinct for a rogue. A billiard table marker brought three billiard balls to the shop and tried to borrow 6s. on them. The assistant was not satisfied with the man's explanation as to how the balls, 'two white and one red', had come into his possession and called the police. The Bench subsequently imposed a fine of 20s., with the alternative of fourteen days' imprisonment, and the Chief Constable announced his intention of impounding the balls 'in the public interest', although the reasoning behind this is a little difficult to follow.[27]

Less acumen was required in order to decide that the police should be called to High Street, Wandsworth in order to arrest Mr Harry Edwards. Mr Edwards, who was very drunk at the time, had called at the pawnshop to offer himself as a pledge. 'The magistrate told the prisoner that, as he was detained at the Police Station instead of the Pawnbroker's, he would have to pay 2s 6d. to redeem himself.'[28]

Not unnaturally, *The Pawnbrokers' Gazette* took every opportunity to draw attention to the community activities and good works undertaken by members of the trade. These items add a pleasant human dimension to what might otherwise have been an unbroken sequence of court cases, technicalities and government measures affecting pawnbrokers. In 1895, for instance:

> Mr J. T. Jackson, a member of the Leeds Trade, who has 27 branches in Lancashire and Yorkshire, and resides at Park House, Pool, near Ilkley, on Friday last gave his Annual Tea and Social Gathering in the Pool Wesleyan Chapel. Whilst about a hundred of the villagers were enjoying tea in the school room, Mr Jackson was at the same time entertaining a number of private friends at his residence at Park House. Among the guests were Sir John Barran, Bart., Member for the Atley Division, and Lady Barran; Alderman and Mrs Scarr, of Leeds; and a number of other well-known ladies and gentlemen. After tea the party adjourned to the chapel, where a lengthy programme was gone through, and which was highly appreciated by all present. Though the gale was raging at the time, the chapel was nearly filled.[29]

A little later in the same month:

> Many different plans have been adopted by the Pawnbroking

fraternity throughout the United Kingdom to provide their numerous customers with a small present as Christmas comes round. But something new has been introduced by Mr Richard Parkin, Pawnbroker and jeweller, 21 Mill-lane, Bentwick, Newcastle-upon-Tyne. The class of people which exist in the district (in which his business is located) is very poor, therefore on Christmas eve he presented fully 500 spice loaves to the most needful in Bentwick. Taking into consideration that he has only been in business for a short period, this is an act of kindness and generosity which should not fail to be recorded, as well as highly appreciated.[30]

The reports of annual dinners make excellent reading. In the spring of 1895, the Wigan Pawnbrokers' Association appear to have done themselves rather well at the town's Ship Hotel. The menu was:

Soup: Clear.
Fish: Cod and Oyster Sauce.
Removes: Roast Beef, Mutton and Chickens. Boiled Chickens. York Ham. Roast Turkey and Sausages.
Pancakes, Plum Pudding, Apple Meringue, Blanc Mange.
Cheese and Salad.[31]

The Benevolent Society of Assistant Pawnbrokers had the habit of holding their dinners at the Holborn Restaurant in London. The dinner was always followed by a concert, the details of which were always reported by the *Gazette*. On one occasion not long before the turn of the century, the programme included two intriguingly titled comic songs rendered by Mr F. Wilson. The first was 'The Sanitary Inspector' and the second, 'It must have been the lobster'. One can only guess at their contents.

A pawnbroker could fairly claim that his work was not lacking in variety. He came into contact with the full range of human behaviour and human types, and years of experience had taught him that nothing was impossible. In 1896 Mr Parritt, of Romford, sent *The Pawnbrokers' Gazette* a list of some of his stranger pledges. Back in 1861, he had lent 6s. on a telescope. For thirty-five years the interest due on the loan had been paid regularly, first by the pledger himself and then, after his death, by his relatives. In 1896 the telescope was redeemed; the few shillings required had not been available until then. Even more remarkable was the case of the pair of sheets which had been pledged fifty years previously for 10s. each. They were still in good condition, although not worth the money that had been lent on them and, once again, the interest had been faithfully paid. Mr Parritt – his name possibly gave him an extra sympathy with cage birds and their owners – had also at one time taken in a canary. The interest had been paid for a year in advance, together with an estimated amount for seed. The canary was not redeemed and the pawnbroker kept it as a pet until it died.[32]

Equally pleasant, but more practical, was the revelation of the commercial traveller that, 'whenever he was in a place and the railway cloakroom was crowded, he always pawned his overcoat and other encumbrances for the day, and could do so as cheaply as leaving them at a railway station'.[33]

Less agreeable, as a reflection of human fecklessness and stupidity, rather than eccentricity, was the case, which occurred in Bolton, of a man who pawned clothing infected with scarlet fever. The clothing was pledged for half-a-crown by the father, who had simply taken the clothes from a pile in a basket. When the mother realised what had happened, she rushed to the pawnshop and redeemed the clothes. At that point, the police were called in and the father was prosecuted and fined. Fortunately, no one else was infected, although, as the magistrate pointed out, a major outbreak could easily have taken place.[34] But such incidents did nothing to help the reputation of a trade which could only suffer by being associated in the public mind, however unfairly, with poverty, disease and crime.

A regrettably high proportion of our fellow citizens, however, do not behave in as sensible a fashion as one might wish and pawnbrokers have perhaps had to deal with more than their fair share of them. They have consequently stood to gain, rather than lose, from legislation which laid down as precisely as possible what the respective obligations of pawnbrokers and their customers were. The 1872 Act was not perfect – no Act ever is – but it was a great improvement on what had existed previously and it provided a remarkably good framework within which a pawnbroker could do business with unbusinesslike people.

The 1872 Act – its main provisions are summarised in Appendix

1 – was the result of considerable pressure on the part of the pawnbrokers themselves, who had suffered from the anomalies and imperfections of the existing legislation controlling their business. In particular, they wanted the Government to introduce a new schedule of profits, and to be allowed to exceed the profits laid down in the schedule by means of special contracts. Broadly speaking, the new Act met their demands. If the sums of money stipulated in it seem ridiculously small today, this is because the inflation of the past twenty years has changed our whole concept of money values. From that point of view, the 1872 Act had become completely antiquated by the time the decision was taken to abandon it and to subject pawnbrokers to the more wide-ranging provisions of the Consumer Credit Act. To do business nowadays, in terms of halfpennies and pennies is laughable, but it still made quite good sense up to the 1950s.

Before the Pawnbrokers' Bill was drafted, a Select Committee of the House of Commons collected evidence over a period of two years. During the debate on the Bill, however, one Member drew the attention of the House to the curious fact that the Select Committee had heard from nobody who had actually made use of the services of a pawnbroker. 'We have not got one piece of evidence,' he said, 'from the lower classes of the people, who deal with the Pawnbrokers, because they would be ashamed to say that they dealt with them.'[35]

An interesting feature of the 1872 Act is that it was prepared and passed before pawnbrokers had a national association to represent them. Many local associations existed, to provide mutual defence and support, those in London and Manchester being especially vigorous, but their efforts were uncoordinated and by the 1870s it had become widely recognised that some form of national body was essential. The early issues of *The Pawnbrokers' Gazette* contain a number of letters advocating such an association, the leading crusader being Alfred Hardaker, a Liverpool man who campaigned for more than twenty years to persuade his colleagues of the need to think in more than local terms. A first meeting of delegates, representing most of the areas of England and Scotland, was held in Derby in 1892, and an Association established, with Hardaker as its Secretary. The first set of rules, drawn up at Derby, had not proved satisfactory, and in 1895 the National Pawnbrokers' Association of Great

71

Britain was reconstituted. It has had a continuous history since that date.

The main weakness of the original rules had been connected with finance. Each affiliated society was required to contribute 2s. 6d. for each of its members, but many local societies felt this was too much and some of them, including the powerful Metropolitan Pawnbrokers' Protection Society, had not joined for this reason. The new scale was calculated to give the Association a minimum annual income of £120, of which £50 was to be placed to reserve. Such a budget seems very small by modern standards, but was apparently sufficient to allow the Association to do excellent work on behalf of its members.

One of its earliest and most valuable functions was to try to persuade more pawnbrokers to insure their premises and their stock. The Goldsmiths' and General Burglary Insurance Association had been founded in 1892, with its headquarters in Gresham Street. Most of the directors were London pawnbrokers and most of the capital had been subscribed by members of the trade. In 1895 it had a premium income of £10,140 15s. 2d., claims of £2,823 11s. 7d., and paid a dividend of 8¾ per cent.

When the Association began its new career in 1895, its Committee included two people who became very important in the pawnbroking world during the first quarter of the twentieth century, Henry Arthur Attenborough, as Chairman, and Walter Bull, as Treasurer. The Secretary was James Sprunt, Alfred Hardaker having retired before his work had come to real fruition. By this time, it was clear that pawnbroking was beginning to shed its early Victorian image. 'The Provincial Pawnbroker,' wrote the *Gazette*, 'is surely, but slowly it may be, making his way in public estimation. The prejudices of the old times die hard, but happily they are quietly disappearing. It was thought a great advance that the late Mr John Colburn was elected Lord Mayor of York; then we had Mr Hart, Mayor of Canterbury; later Mr Cooke, at Hanley; Mr Boulton, for Stoke; Mr Fraser, at Ipswich; Mr Willis, at Rochester; and several others. Then came that important appointment of Mr Goolden, as Sheriff of Newcastle. Now we have Mr Shaw, Mayor of Birkenhead; and not to endeavour to enumerate Magistrates, Aldermen and Town Councillors. It must be admitted, that there can exist no popular prejudice against members of the Trade occupying representative positions.'[36]

As part of the campaign to present pawnbrokers as solid, public-spirited citizens, the *Gazette* printed, during the 1890s, a series of profiles of leading pawnbrokers in various parts of the country. Councillor James Thompson, of Salford, was a typical example.[37] Born in Salford in 1842, he joined the Army when he was seventeen and served for twenty-one years, rising to the rank of first-class staff sergeant. He began business as a pawnbroker in his native Salford in 1880, and by 1896 he had, in addition to his original shop, 'a large, seamen's outfitting establishment' near the Ship Canal Docks, in Trafford Road, a second pawnbroking shop also in Trafford Road, and a drapery business in Irlam. Since 1892 he had been a member of Salford Town Council, being 'an active worker on the water, finance, town hall and markets, baths, and cemetery committees', and a member of the Salford Board of Guardians. 'He is,' wrote the author of the *Gazette* article, 'an Englishman of the thorough John Bull type, and his actions are characterised by a strict integrity of purpose and honesty.'

But this sterling image was not accepted everywhere. Mr James A. Radcliffe, of Birkenhead, had made efforts to open a branch in Southport, but abandoned the attempt after finding that 'there was a deepseated prejudice in the minds of the inhabitants, police and magistrates of the fashionable little watering place being lowered and disgraced by the insignia of "My Uncle".'[38]

NOTES

1 William Weir, *The First Hundred Years, 1851–1951*: a sketch of the history of the Glasgow Pawnbrokers' Association, 1951, p. 15.
2 Ibid, p. 18.
3 *Manchester and Salford Co-operative Herald*, August 1904, p. 135.
4 *Manchester Gazette*, 5 May 1914.
5 However, a note in *The Pawnbrokers' Gazette* for 4 March 1872 says there were, at this time, 400 pawnbrokers in London, each with five or six assistants.
6 17 December 1870.
7 *The Times*, 23 December 1870.
8 Vol. II, p. 110. Reprinted 1968 by Dover Publications, from the original 1861–2 edition. See also David Macrae, *The Social Hydra, or the Influences of the Traffic of Pawnbrokers and Brokers on the Religious, Moral and Social Condition of the Working Classes and the Poor*, 1861. Macrae refers to pawnbroking as 'offensive to the moral sense of the Scotch'.
9 Op. cit., Vol. IV, pp. 289–90.
10 18 January 1865.
11 *The Times*, 19 January 1865.
12 *The Illustrated London News*, 31 July 1852.
13 *The Illustrated London News*, 20 July 1861.
14 The case is described in *The Illustrated London News*, 11 April 1885.
15 *The Illustrated London News*, 19 April 1879.
16 *The Illustrated London News*, 18 January 1864.
17 *The Illustrated London News*, 27 February 1864.
18 *The Illustrated London News*, 27 December 1873.
19 *The Illustrated London News*, 20 December 1873.
20 *The Illustrated London News*, 18 January 1868.
21 *The Illustrated London News*, 4 November 1871.
22 *The Illustrated London News*, 1 November 1873.
23 *The Pawnbrokers' Gazette and Trade Circular*, 11 November 1872.
24 *The Pawnbrokers' Gazette*, 8 January 1872.
25 *Leeds Mercury*, 19 January 1895.
26 *The Pawnbrokers' Gazette*, 18 November 1872.
27 *The Pawnbrokers' Gazette*, 22 August 1896.
28 *The Pawnbrokers' Gazette*, 6 April 1895.
29 *The Pawnbrokers' Gazette*, 5 January 1895.
30 *The Pawnbrokers' Gazette*, 12 January 1895.
31 *The Pawnbrokers' Gazette*, 3 March 1895.
32 *The Pawnbrokers' Gazette*, 4 July 1896.
33 *The Pawnbrokers' Gazette*, 4 April 1896.
34 *The Pawnbrokers' Gazette*, 2 May 1896.
35 Reported in *The Pawnbrokers' Gazette*, 18 July 1872.
36 *The Pawnbrokers' Gazette*, 12 January 1895.
37 *The Pawnbrokers' Gazette*, 19 September 1896.
38 *The Pawnbrokers' Gazette*, Letter in issue of 11 March 1872.

5

The Early Twentieth Century

With the twentieth century, we have arrived at the period when we are no longer dependent entirely on written evidence. The old people whose first-hand experiences are so important to the historian are still alive to talk to us. We can meet the veteran pawn-brokers and their customers and use their reminiscences to check the information we find in print. And the more opportunities of this kind that come our way, the more we are likely to regret their absence for the earlier periods. The written word may give us the basic facts; the spoken word provides the flavour, the balance and the subtleties. A careful combination of the two gives us a reasonable chance of understanding what actually happened.

The oral historian always wishes, however, that it had been possible for him to begin his enquiries ten years earlier. Old people have an unfortunate habit of dying before one has had a chance to meet them. One sometimes forgets that anyone who was ten in 1900 would be over ninety today, and there are not a great many people of that age still around. For all practical purposes, 1914, the year when the First World War broke out, is now the earliest date for which we are likely to be able to collect first-hand reminiscences in any quantity. This makes someone like Jesse White of Bristol a jewel beyond price, a collector's item, because in 1981 Mr White was a hale and hearty 85, very much with all his wits about him.

He went to work for a pawnbroker in Barton Hill, Bristol, in 1910, when he was fourteen. Most of the people in the area worked in the local cotton factory, where wages were even lower than in the textile districts of Lancashire. Jesse White's father was an iron-moulder, earning five pounds a week, which was good money for

75

the time, and his mother was paid one pound a week as a warper in the Great Western Cotton Mill. It was a large family, and from about the age of twelve the children were expected to earn whatever they could outside school hours. The young Jesse White found a part-time job with a local pawnbroker and when he left school he went there full-time. This is how he remembers the work and the place:

I worked Friday nights and Saturdays all day for 1s. 6d. a week. Eventually I got a 3d. rise. My work was in the warehouse. We had 500–600 customers on a Monday. They were very poor and ill-educated. Half of them couldn't read or write. They had to cover their expenses the best way they could. Some went to the pubs over the weekend and were broke by Sunday evening, so on Monday morning they came to the pawnbroker. The educated man could go to the bank and ask for a few pounds; poor people with families to bring up went to the pawnbroker. It was always the women who came. They brought their husbands' suits, shoes, wedding rings, all sorts of things, and on that they raised sufficient money to carry on for the week.

The man I worked for was John Swaish. He had five other shops and became Sir John Swaish, Lord Mayor of Bristol. He lived in Clifton.[1] The six shops weren't all the same. There were three levels of pawnbroking, low, medium and high. It depended on the district. Ours was low, but it was a very smart, clean, well-equipped shop. Us boys in the warehouse had to keep it perfectly clean. There were eight of us working there – two boys writing the tickets, one man taking in the pledges, another fellow doing up the articles as he dealt with them and valued them, the man round the corner paying out, and the rest of us in the warehouse. The warehouse at Barton Hill was a three-storey brick building, where he kept thousands of parcels and bundles.

People used to pledge things for half-a-crown, 1s. 6d., 9d. even, which was money in those days. You could get a meal for four or five kids for that. In Barton Hill people used to do their washing on the Monday, plenty of it, and they'd pay a woman 3d., perhaps 6d., to bring their washing in and pledge it for the week. One particular woman, I remember, had a little handcart and she came every week with this loaded up with people's washing.[2]

Jesse White still has vivid memories of being shown, as an apprentice, how to cut a tight ring off the finger of the wearer – it was a simple but skilful task. On one never-to-be-forgotten occasion he was required to go to a house in order to cut off a ring and found on arrival that the woman was in the process of having a baby. He removed the ring, as he had been instructed to do, and departed to arrange the much-needed loan on it.

The reminiscences of the elderly, although nearly always full of interesting information, need to be used and interpreted with caution. The past is sometimes seen through a rosy haze and, over the years, a story can have been retold, polished and rehearsed so often that a listener may well find himself being presented with something which, if not exactly fiction, is at least a greatly improved version of the truth. But if, on the other hand, several members of the same generation make the same point, there is every reason to believe it is true. A useful approach is often to ask the person one is interviewing what he knows or thinks about a piece of information one has come across in one's reading or in the course of a conversation with someone else. And not infrequently a completely new and perhaps important line of enquiry can be started as a result of a chance remark made in a discussion.

Charles Allsopp is in his eighties, a year or two younger than Jesse White and a fellow Bristolian. If their memories of pawnbroking in Bristol at the beginning of the century are substantially the same, one is entitled to believe that one is being given an accurate account of the situation.

Mr Allsopp entered the trade just as Mr White did.

We were very poor and Mother had to use the pawnbroker. She came back one day and said, 'The boy's left. He wants a boy. Would you like the job? Go up and see.' So I did. The pawnbroker was J. B. H. Baker and he said, 'All right. You can start.' And I'll tell you what my start was. First of all, the boy had to clean the windows, sweep the shop out, make sure the door was open for the customers and get the books ready. We used to have a big thick book and we made two entries in it and two on a pawn ticket, which we tore in half. Half was given to the customer. It said what she'd pledged and how much she'd

77

borrowed on it. The other half was pinned to the parcel, with the number. My job was to see to all that and make sure the customers were happy.[3]

He enjoyed the work and got on well with the people.

They were an enjoyment in themselves, the customers. They were mostly women. If men came, they usually caused trouble, because the women always used to pawn their husbands' suits on Monday, to get the money for the week's rent. If the husband had an appointment that week, he wanted his suit. But it was in pawn and she had no money to get it out, so he used to start knocking her about. There was a law then, that if the husband went to the pawnbroker and said, 'Don't take anything else in from my wife,' the pawnbroker had to do that. If he hadn't got the money to pay the rent without pawning his suit, she went to the Guardians, and they helped as a rule.

When the suit was new, the pawnbroker would probably lend a pound on it, but as it got worn the amount went steadily down, so that eventually it was worth practically nothing. When that happened, the man usually went to a credit trader, who was always known as the duffer. He got a new suit and agreed to pay for it at the rate of a shilling a week. It was years before the loan was paid off, and quite often the people concerned never bothered, knowing the courts would never help the duffer to get his money back.

The pawnbroker, said Mr Allsopp, was a necessary part of the lives of poor people. It was the only way they could live. He instanced his own mother. Her husband was a seaman, paid eight pounds a month, together with an allowance of four pounds a month for the wife. On this Mrs Allsopp was supposed to keep six children, which was clearly impossible, even for a woman who ran her home as cheaply as she possibly could. If she happened to drink, as many of them did, the situation was disastrous.

The pawnshop where Charles Allsopp worked was in Lower Ashley Road, immediately opposite the 'Lord Nelson' public house, where many of the shop's customers were in the habit of spending their Friday and Saturday evenings, forgetting about the need to pay the pawnbroker a visit, so that they could redeem their goods for the weekend. The pawnbroker, as Mr Allsopp remembers, was extremely accommodating. 'I had to go over to the pub at twelve o'clock – they were there drinking gin and this and that –

and tell them, "Look, we're shutting now." That was twelve o'clock on a Saturday night.'

Not all the customers were poor people. Some of them – but Mr Allsopp insists it was a very small proportion of the total – were what was known higher up the social scale as temporarily inconvenienced.

We used to get occasional persons on business, who'd run a bit short and had to find the money quick. They used to come down and pledge their best jewellery, £200 of it sometimes, to pay a bill. One of our most regular customers of this sort was a furniture maker. When he first started up in Bristol, he didn't have a lot of money, and he often used to come to us when there was a bill to meet. He had some lovely jewellery and he'd be borrowing hundreds of pounds on it.

Even the deeds of a house we took in one day. Things like this were really pledged for safety, not just for the money. A lot of people came to us before they went away on holiday. They used to pledge their jewellery with us, because it was the cheapest way of making sure it was safe. An insurance premium would have cost them much more. Our charge was only fivepence in the pound a month, and you could leave £500 worth of jewellery and borrow only a pound on it, because, for this type of customer, the loan wasn't the important thing.

Charles Allsopp fell out with Mr Baker on one occasion and took a job in Ebbw Vale, a step he soon regretted. Baker of Bristol had always made a point of observing the law in its smallest details, but Ebbw Vale turned out to be very different. Among his other peccadilloes, the pawnbroker there had the habit of withholding half-a-crown of the pledge money and giving his unfortunate customers half-a-pound of tea instead, which was, of course, completely illegal. Not wanting to be involved in such behaviour, Mr Allsopp soon returned to the rectitude of Bristol and Mr Baker.

During the 1914–18 war, pawnbrokers were forced to employ women as assistants and some of them continued to work in the trade after the war had ended. One who did was Mrs E. P. Kidd of Gateshead. She started in 1914. She was paid the almost unbelievably low wage of 3s. a week to begin with and had to work 48 hours a week to earn it. It was a large business, with nine branches, and Mrs Kidd eventually rose to become manageress of one of them. Until the early Twenties, she remembers, customers were very poor.

Mr T. J. Ottaway, who now lives in Devon, did part-time work for a London pawnbroker for two years, 1915 and 1916, while he was still at school. The shop was in London, in the Borough High Street, and he found the work extremely interesting. In term-time he worked in the evenings and on Saturdays, and during holidays he was there all day and every day, starting at eight in the morning and carrying on until at least eleven at night. For these enormous hours he received 8s. 6d. a week, which was a great deal better than Mrs Kidd achieved in Gateshead, but still, one feels, an excellent bargain for his employers.[4]

On pledge days[5] [he remembers], I operated the ticket-writing machine, which did three tickets at once.[6] I also helped with wrapping goods which needed to be wrapped and fixing tickets to the parcels. Then I helped to get all the parcels up by rope and pulley to the store-rooms above. In the warehouse we had no gas or electric lighting, but there were huge colza-oil lamps that showed us where the parcels were.[7]

There were certain advantages attached to the job. There was the usual retail shop attached to the pawnbrokers. Mr Ottaway remembers buying a couple of articles at the request of his school-teacher, who knew he worked there. But, when the time came for him to leave school at fourteen, he decided not to stay in pawnbroking. His decision had nothing to do with hours, wages, or any dislike of work. 'I left,' he admitted, 'mainly because my pals used to go to the pictures on Saturday afternoons, while I had to work.'

Mr G. H. Mobbs was brought up in pawnshops in the East End of London, first in one his father managed and afterwards in premises which belonged to the family. The surroundings, the customers, and the details of a pawnbroker's life made a permanent and deep impression on him. A mental catalogue of the pledged goods still runs through his mind – 'Best shoes and clothes; sheets, often new from the tally-man; suits; the daughter's dance dress; watches and rings; bundles of assorted clean clothes, pledged for any amount from 1s. 6d. to 10s.; a few "better items" – a type-writer, books, vases.'[8]

The customers were 'poor East End women of all ages, who came in weekly, usually with the same pledges. I didn't see the better off or occasional customer, who was dealt with in the "front shop". The ordinary run of customers used the side entrance and had no privacy at all.'

Mr Mobbs himself lent a hand in the shop during his spare time, stacking and looking out parcels, writing tickets on the machine – 'no doubt I was more literate than an employed boy', sweeping up the shop, cleaning windows, collecting dropped pins with a magnet. All this came to an end at the age of thirteen and a half, when he transferred to a grammar school, 'and the family moved to a more salubrious area'. For his father, however, the new home in the suburbs meant an extension of his already long working day. 'My father,' he recalls, 'never spent a weekend at the seaside in the summer, as Monday and Saturday were the big days, and he couldn't leave the work to his assistants. Because the shops were in a poor quarter, someone had to be in the building all night, in case the locals broke in. When we ourselves were no longer living over one or other of the shops, a housekeeper or a resident manager had to be in occupation.'

Mrs Betty Saunders, formerly of Plumstead Road, Woolwich, and now in Devon, has a very similar story to tell. Her father, whose name was Fowler, was born in the Gray's Inn Road area of London in 1883 and became a pawnbroker's shop boy when he was fourteen. His employers were Harvey & Thompson, who had a number of branches in London, and he was one of several boys at this particular branch. They all lived in, sleeping on camp beds actually in the shop. Mr Fowler stayed the course and by 1911, the year in which he married, he had become manager of the firm's Leather Lane branch. The building is still there, a splendid late Victorian edifice which has since been divided up into separate business premises. One part, however, is still a jeweller's and pawnbroker's, and still part of Harvey & Thompson. Pawnbroking, like any other industry, has its archaeology, which is well worth studying.

My mother [says Mrs Saunders], took on the task of supervising the domestic life, not only of herself and my father, but of six 'living-in' boys, on the staff of the shop. Conditions were better than they had been for my father in his young days. These boys had a proper dormitory in the large and quite handsome 'upstairs' accommodation, and my mother had a resident maid, paid for by the firm, to help her with the cooking and house-keeping. In fact, my mother's mother was also employed by Harvey & Thompson as a 'living-in help', so pawnbroking must have been a prosperous business in those days.

I wasn't born until 1921, so I haven't any personal memories of those days, only family talk. I remember stories of the extensive 'carriage trade' that was done in Leather Lane, with the nobility and gentry appearing in person to pawn their gold and silver and luxuries of all kinds. Leather Lane wasn't far from the West End, of course. All the time my father was manager there, the hours of work were very long for everybody concerned. So far as I was able to gather, the shop stayed open while there were potential customers in the street.

During the 1914–18 war, my father and all the young men on the staff were away in the Army, and the business was carried on mainly by women and girls. My father's health was badly affected by the mustard gas attacks he'd been through in France, and he was evidently thought by the directors of Harvey & Thompson to be unfit to be in charge of their most important branch, so he was demoted to New Cross. He and my mother resented this – New Cross did quite a different class of business – and they eventually left Harvey & Thompson's altogether, and my father eventually, in 1924, became manager of Earl's Stores in Woolwich. This was by no means a step up in the pawnbroking trade.

We shall be continuing Mrs Saunders's reminiscences in the next chapter, but meanwhile it is interesting to compare the pawnbroking world as she knew it in the first quarter of the present century with two items of personal history published in *The Times*, the first in 1961 and the second in 1957.

Both articles were anonymous, an interesting sidelight on the attitude which so many people had and have towards an activity which was a normal and regular part of the lives not only of working-class people, but, as Mrs Saunders mentions above, of the 'carriage trade' as well. A feeling of shame evidently lingered long after the incidents described took place. So far as *The Times* was concerned, pawnbroking was a quaint, old-fashioned activity, a period piece. For the two authors, however, it was something to be remembered and written about with caution.

The first article, 'Life Among the Pledges: Childhood Memories of a Victorian Pawnbroker's Daughter', was written from the privileged side of the pawnbroking fence, the side on which pawnbroking could be fun for children, a giant toy-cupboard and perpetual Christmas party.

It must have been in 1890 [the pawnbroker's daughter reminisces], that we went to live over the shop, and even though my elder sister and I felt very much ashamed when, at school, we had to give our address or say what our father's occupation was, our memories of our years there are happy ones. For one thing we were a typically Victorian and therefore expanding family; there were six of us children when we first went to the shop and nine by the time we left, and there was so much space there, for we lived not only 'over the shop', but under and around it.

Below in the basement was a huge kitchen, with cellars behind where some of the pledges were stored – not very interesting ones we thought – fenders, fire-irons, tool-boxes, spades and the like. On the ground floor was the shop, a long narrow place, everlastingly gaslit and festooned with unredeemed pledges of all kinds, where Dad, with two assistants and two or three apprentices, carried on his business as pawnbroker and jeweller.

On the first floor were a family sitting-room and bedrooms, and above, in the attics, were two warehouses, one for clothing and the other – a fascinating place to us – for ornaments, curios and musical instruments. Though we were told not to touch any of these valuable things we willingly risked Dad's wrath to play with or on the mandolines, guitars, banjos, concertinas and melodeons that found a temporary resting place there.

The shop itself we saw less of, though all our lives revolved round it. From Monday to Friday it was open from 8 a.m. until 8 p.m., and on Saturdays it never closed before 11 p.m., while often work went on up till almost midnight. The apprentices no longer lived in – my father during his apprenticeship slept under the counter in the traditional way – but they were almost part of the family, having a hasty dinner with us in the kitchen, still in their shirt-sleeves and shiny black aprons between spells

83

of 'watching the shop', for there was no midday closing then.

The shop had two entrances, one leading to the sale counter, which was open, and the other to the pledge counter, which was divided off by partitions so that shy customers could not see one another. At one end of the pledge counter was a desk where one of the assistants made out pawn tickets in duplicate, one ticket for the client and the other for an apprentice to pin or stick to the pledge, and entered each transaction in a huge ledger. And behind the counter stood huge racks; in these the bundles of clothing, carefully wrapped in dust sheets, and bearing on one end their numbered tickets, were ranged in order, and when the racks were full the apprentices carried them up to the warehouse in the attic.

Saturday nights and Monday mornings were, of course, the busiest times. On Mondays the women brought in their family's Sunday best – the husband's suit, boots, and often his watch and chain, the girls' frocks, the boys' sailor suits, their own dresses, shoes and shawls – and commonly the whole of the family wash, clean, dried and ironed, for storage until the next weekend.

Most of these things were carefully folded and wrapped in dust sheets, but (for an extra penny) dresses could be put on a hanger. I never remember seeing a hat brought in, though during the week temporarily embarrassed housewives would come in with all kinds of other things – clocks, ornaments and pieces of furniture, sheets, rugs, carpets and blankets, even wedding rings and flat-irons.

The Saturday, the day when most of the pledges were redeemed, was the day my sister and I looked forward to most. The shop was so busy that we were called in to help (from dinner-time until 10 p.m.) and got a shilling each for our labours, which seemed like riches to us then.

Our job was up in the clothing attic, which was connected to the shop by a rope and chute. The rope was tied to a bell at our end and had a canvas bag at the other; the chute ran from one corner of the attic to the shop counter itself. When the bell rang we pulled up the rope and took the tickets out of the bag. Then we found the corresponding bundles in the racks and dropped them into the chute, and whoosh! they slid down, right past our living quarters and out into Dad's waiting hands on the counter.

This simple device always seemed to us wonderful and amusing. Our giggling helped to pass away the time, and further variety was provided when apprentices had to come up to get something from the other attic – a trombone or a lacquered cabinet or a bronze statuette, perhaps – and we would persuade them to fetch us a pennyworth of toffee or of chips on their next visit.[9]

A child whose family went to the pawnshop from sheer necessity was likely to have rather different memories of it all. The author of 'Pawnshop and Tallyman During a Lambeth Childhood'[10] had very clear memories of his mother's carefully worked out system of household management, an ingenious combination of 'tallying' and pawning. She would pay 5s. to the representative of a finance company, popularly known as the 'tallyman'. Having done this, she was given a clothing 'cheque' for five pounds, i.e. twenty times the first instalment, which she used to buy clothes for one or more of her five children. The children were allowed to wear the clothes for a day or two, and then the pawnshop had them. Great care was taken to prevent one's neighbours knowing that one was going to the pawnshop. A child never forgets this kind of adventure.

> There were even occasions, if my mother felt that the neighbours suspected that she was visiting the pawnshop, when a penny tram ride would be taken in a direction away from the pawnshop, and from the alighting point a devious journey made back through side streets to the real destination.
> The policeman on traffic duty at the crossroads just by the pawnshop knew my mother well by sight, and as soon as she arrived at the crossroads would hold up the traffic so that she could cross in safety, at the same time wishing her good luck with her pledges in the 'pop shop'.
> Inside the pawnshop were cubicles, and only when she was there in the half light in one of them did my mother really relax and feel safe from detection by the 'neighbours'. But she had a great experience once when a respected neighbour arrived, with a similar aim, in the same cubicle as herself.

These clothes were essentially articles to be pawned, not worn. They were part of the family's financial capital and, since they were pawned on a Monday and taken out on a Saturday, they were not available for the children to wear to school during the week. On one occasion, however, the mother was not well enough to go to the pawnshop on Monday, so that her son, the author of *The Times* article, was allowed to wear the overcoat and boots to school on the Monday, Tuesday and Wednesday. On Thursday, the clothes were back in the pawnshop again, with consequences the unfortunate victim was unlikely to forget.

> I arrived at school on this bitter winter's day without an overcoat and in canvas shoes, and stood shivering and almost crying with cold in the playground. The teacher asked me, as I looked so cold, why was I not wearing my overcoat and where were my boots. Pride forbade me to tell her the real reason, so I said I did not need them as my (old and out-at-elbows) jersey was warm enough. The teacher said: 'Stupid boy, leaving your overcoat and boots at home, you deserve to be cold.'

The tallyman received, when he was able to get the money, a shilling a week for twenty-one weeks for every pound's worth of goods bought. Since the pawnbroker also had to be paid his charges, anyone who arranged their affairs in this curious and complicated way would not appear to be behaving very sensibly. Yet, as her son recalled, this particular financial genius got along quite well, justifying her technique by constantly reminding herself that 'Nobody's really hard up while they have something to pawn'. The fact that she was pawning goods not yet paid for seemed to bother her not at all.

Within one's local community there were certain clearly understood conventions in the matter of pawning. In Salford at the beginning of this century one's social position depended not only on what one possessed, but also on what one pawned.[11] It was low not to take one's best clothes out of pawn in order to wear them on a Sunday, low to pawn furniture or domestic equipment. 'Inability to redeem basic goods was a sure sign of a family's approaching destitution, and credit dried up fast in local tick shops. Naturally, the gulf between those households who patronised "Uncle", even if only occasionally, and those who did not gaped wide. Some families would go hungry rather than pawn their belongings.'[12]

The pawnshop could be and was used in ways which would hardly have occurred to the more affluent members of society.

During the First World War, the Liquor Control Board made attempts to cut down heavy drinking at the weekend, on the very reasonable grounds that it interfered with industrial production and consequently handicapped the war effort. One of the Board's measures was to prohibit the sale of spirits for consumption off the premises between 2.30 p.m. on Friday and noon on Monday. The British working-man is nothing if not ingenious and what he did was to buy a supply of gin or whisky immediately he was paid on a Friday and then take it, not to his home, where it would all have gone by Saturday at the latest, but to the pawnshop. Here it used to be pledged for a small sum and here it was safe, to be taken out piecemeal during the next few days as required.

After *The Times* had written an article describing and regretting the practice,[13] the National Pawnbrokers' Association wrote an indignant letter to the paper. The contents of the article were, said the Association, 'a complete surprise' to their Council and members. They were 'entirely opposed' to the practice. The letter, signed by the President, Walter Bull, and the Hon. Secretary, Sidney Smith, continued as follows:

> Pawnbrokers, as a body, have loyally assisted in every way to carry out the wishes of the powers that be for the welfare of the country in these troubled times, and we feel confident that the practice referred to by your correspondent, if it exists at all, is very limited. However, as he states that a pawnbroker has told him such is the case we have this morning written to our trade journal, *The Pawnbrokers' Gazette*, asking for the assistance of every pawnbroker in the United Kingdom to assist in making impossible this means of evading the spirit of the liquor regulations, and we feel sure this request will meet with a ready and complete response.[14]

It was exceptional for the Association to take this kind of action among its members, and indeed it had no power to compel anyone to do anything. Its function was to advise, to inform and to co-ordinate, a policy which was reflected year by year in the style and contents of its official publication, *The Pawnbrokers' Gazette*. In the years immediately following the death of Queen Victoria, the general tone of its articles can hardly be described as optimistic. Pawnbroking, it believed, was on the decline, if decline was to be measured in terms of the number of pawnshops per ten thousand of the population. In 1902 it noted that 'throughout the United Kingdom and more particularly in large industrial centres like London and Glasgow . . . while the population has been steadily increasing, there has been no corresponding increase in the number of Pawnbroking Offices.'[15]

This reasoning is not necessarily sound. The prosperity of an industry cannot be judged merely on the basis of the number of firms in it, nor the size of its labour force. On the contrary, a smaller number of larger, better sited and more efficiently run shops could well have made more money for those who had invested their capital in the trade.

In 1905 the Birmingham Pawnbrokers' Association organised a debate, the subject for discussion being, 'Is Pawnbroking on the Decline?'[16] It produced considerable disagreement among the members present, mainly, one suspects, because not everyone interpreted 'decline' in the same way. To some it meant a decline in the number of individual businesses, to others a decline in the volume of trade, to others a decline in the number of customers, and to others again a decline in profitability. One speaker thought that there was far too much conservative thinking among his fellow pawnbrokers. The chances of individual pawnbrokers, he felt, were not the same as they were thirty years earlier. Pawnbrokers, like other traders, were being affected by the growth of large combines, but he saw nothing sinister or strange about this. He believed that he could detect a steady improvement in the morale of the trade as a whole. The improvement in education had made customers sharper in realising what interest they were paying and consequently more discriminating in their pledging. This could, he admitted, often be to the disadvantage of the pawnbroker, but other kinds of business could easily say the same. He was afraid, he said, that what he called 'the suspicious element that lurked in the corner of pawnbrokers' offices' was to a great extent fostered by those members of the trade 'who carried on their calling in a slipshod fashion'.

It may very well have been so. Any trade or professional association is always in the difficult position of having to present its members as paragons to the outside world, while knowing at the same time that some of them are progressive and eager to apply new ideas, while others, possibly the majority, resent change and ask for nothing more than a quiet life. Paradoxically, many of those who said pawnbroking was in decline may, without realising it, have meant exactly the reverse. Change is not at all the same as decline, although to some people it may feel that way.

Whatever the situation may have been fifty or a hundred years earlier, pawnbroking was not a get-rich-quick business in Edwardian times. But, in good hands, it was a steady, reliable business, offering satisfactory, if not spectacular returns. The annual reports of the pawnbroking firms which had taken advantage of the Limited Liability Companies Acts to form themselves into corporate companies shows this quite clearly. The earliest such company was the Aberdeen Loan Company Ltd, which was set up in 1879, and during the first twenty years of the present century the best known and the largest was Harvey & Thompson Ltd, which, year after year, declared a dividend of between ten and twelve per cent.

Some pawnbrokers at least were showing a determination to break away from the dreary, poverty-stricken image which the Association was anxious the trade should outgrow. One such pioneer was in Scotland. In 1905 the Glasgow Association sent the *Gazette* this report.

> A new office – and one of the finest and most up-to-date in the city – has been opened at 347 Gairbraid Street, Maryhill, by Mr John Waterston, well-known and highly esteemed in the Trade as an active member for some years past of the Executive Committee of the Glasgow Protective Association. Mr Waterston has been his own architect, the arrangement of office and warehouse being planned by himself – with the most satisfactory results. The fittings are all of the very latest pattern, with special boxes and racks and other useful accessories for the storing of goods. Then the electric light is fitted into the place, and it is otherwise – with glass doors, etc. – splendidly lighted, and indeed everything possible has been done to have the office equipped in first rate style for the business of up-to-date Pawnbroking.[17]

But it would be idle to pretend that such attractive and efficient premises were the norm, even by 1930. Too many proprietors were content to run an old-fashioned business in an old-fashioned way, always willing to put the blame for bad results on the state of the economy rather than on themselves.

One of the most interesting features of *The Pawnbrokers' Gazette* was its series of regular reports from the regions. A pawnbroker's business, it appeared, was subject to the most extraordinary influences. In 1902, for example, the Lancashire pawnbrokers reported a poor year, due partly to the industrial depression and partly, surprising as this may seem, to the Boer War. 'From this district,' they said, 'a great number of men – regulars, reservists and volunteers – went to the front and ere they went pawned all the clothing they thought would be of no use to them on the *veldt*. Most of these pledges have remained unredeemed and many of them are proving, so to speak, "of no use to anyone but the owner". Again, owing to the prolongation of hostilities, the men who went out are being detained in South Africa instead of coming home and beginning work here – a fact which means much in relation to the business of the Pawnbroker.'[18]

Over the country as a whole, the sales of jewellery slumped during the months which followed the death of Queen Victoria, but not in Cardiff, which had presented a much brighter picture. 'With regard to articles of jewellery,' the *Gazette* told its readers, 'those offered for pledge have been of a better value than has been known for the past two or three years. This is no doubt attributable to the high wages earned by the colliers . . . They have spent freely in the purchase of articles of adornment, which during periods of holiday making have in many cases found their way to the Pawnbroker.'[19]

The analyst of the ups and downs of pawnbroking had to possess a profound knowledge of local affairs. 1904 was a disappointing year for pawnbrokers in Manchester. 'The engineering trade has been bad, and disputes have occurred in several industries. All these things have a tendency to seriously interfere with the trade of the district . . . Money having been scarce and work in many instances at a standstill, people have not had money to buy new things with, and consequently they have been short of good things on which to raise a little emergency capital. Therefore the pledge counter has not had as many customers as could have been desired and redemptions have been at a discount.'[20]

A special report for the Harpurhey district of the city showed an even worse situation there. 'I think all the Pawnbrokers of Harpurhey are complaining that owing to the short time in the mills, workshops, works, etc., men have only been working three or four days a week, which has caused great poverty in the district. Customers have had to pledge goods in order to live on the money, and those goods will never be redeemed unless trade in general revives. Pledges are heavy, redemptions small in comparison and sales are quiet.'[21]

Dublin appeared to be operating against the general trend and pawnbroking continued to be in a buoyant condition there despite the 'widespread and general distress', which was affecting all classes. The number of pledges made during 1904 was about five million, and the money advanced 'amounted to about £1,000,000'.[22] The *Gazette* reporter in trying to discover why pawnbrokers there were doing so exceptionally well suggested that it was because 'most of the Dublin offices are now owned by a younger generation of new blood and fresh vigour who are leaving old methods behind and are keeping abreast of the times', but, unfortunately, he gave no details as to what these new methods were. But if the figures can be taken as reliable, pawnbroking in Ireland was on a rising wave. The returns for 1906 show that Dublin had 4,516,941 pledges in that year, Belfast 2,410,189, and Cork 613,297. The average amount of each pledge for the whole country, however, was low. A total of nearly twelve million pledges yielded £1¾ million in advances, or less than three shillings a pledge.

The worthies of the trade continued to die off and their obituaries show the continuation of the type of highly respectable public figure described in the previous chapter. Alderman Tom Nixon of Sheffield died in 1910. Born in 1854, he had established himself as a jeweller and pawnbroker with two shops in Sheffield, one in Doncaster and one in Buxton. He had been elected to Sheffield City Council in 1887 and became a magistrate in 1897. He was a director of Sheffield Wednesday Football Club and of the Sheffield Billposting Company, the founder and Vice-President of the Sheffield Crimean and Indian Mutiny Veterans' Association, a member of the Pawnbrokers' General Council, and a Freemason of long standing.[23]

Alderman John Goolden of Newcastle began studying to become a lawyer, but for some unexplained reason he abandoned the law and established a jewellery and pawnbroking shop, which in time became one of the principal businesses in the district. He served for twenty years on the City Council and became Mayor of Newcastle. He was a Justice of the Peace and one of the founders of the National Pawnbrokers' Association, being its President for two years. 'An extremely likeable man,' said his obituary, 'he was natural and cordial in his deportment, could be at ease with anyone and make all others at ease with him. Extremely resolute, he hung on to things he undertook with all the tenacity of a bulldog and none of its ferocity.'[24]

Aldermen Nixon and Goolden were, it will have been noticed, both magistrates. The Association had reason to believe that during the previous quarter of a century no fewer than seventy pawnbrokers had been elected to the Bench and it therefore came as a great surprise to discover, in 1908, that the Lord Chancellor had issued a quiet ruling that in future no member of the pawnbroking trade was to be appointed to the Bench. No public statement to this effect was ever made, but its results became apparent and the Association was annoyed, taking the ban to be a slur on the reputation of its members. During the following twenty years a number of representations were made, first to the Royal Commission on the Selection of JPs in 1910 and then at various times to the Lord Chancellor's office. No satisfactory answer was ever received, but a number of pawnbrokers continued to become magistrates despite the ruling. Their names were apparently submitted in connection with their other business interests. A jeweller or an outfitter was perfectly acceptable as a candidate, even if a pawnbroker was not.

The Association was always on the watch for any unpleasant remarks about the trade, or insinuations that its members were in some way not as other men. In 1912 there was the case of the novel *Christina* by a lady called L. G. Moberley. In the course of her story, Mrs Moberley had a scene describing a visit to a pawnbroker. The proprietor of the business was described in most unflattering terms – 'his fat, sleek countenance'; 'with an odious leer'; 'those underbred, meanspirited curs who regard any defenceless woman as lawful prey'. The pawnbroker's assistants were not well thought of, either. They were dismissed as 'bumptious'. The Association understandably protested, saying that it was obvious that Mrs Moberley had met very few, if any, pawnbrokers and that her prejudice was based on ignorance and possibly malice as well.[25]

Punches were not pulled when the Association set about the task of defending its members. In 1905 there was a leading article[26] on the ignorance that journalists displayed in the matter of pawnbrokers. It had been occasioned by an editorial in a Cardiff newspaper by a leading local solicitor, Lloyd Meyrick.

Locally he may be well-known [said the *Gazette*], but he knows very little about Pawnbroking outside his own locality. With self-complacent superiority he states 'he has not a word to say against Pawnbrokers', yet their shops are 'the resort of the waster' to which 'a stream of poor, broken and vicious humanity' wends its way. To him, apparently, the Welsh border is the uttermost ends of the earth, and what is the custom of the principality is the custom of the world. How, otherwise, can we account for his dictum, 'that it is a Trade that only one race can work well'? 'The Eternal Jew', as Mr Meyrick is pleased to call him, certainly monopolises Pawnbroking in Cardiff and other cities and towns in Wales, but in England and Scotland it is quite an exceptional thing to find a member of the race engaged in the Trade. Yet some of the Gentiles work it well.

Pawnbrokers' assistants were less well organised than their employers. They had their own Benevolent Society, which had been established in the 1860s, and which did excellent work in relieving hardship and misfortune. The following appeal illustrates the type of case with which the Society had to deal.

To the Subscribers of the Benevolent Society of Assistant Pawnbrokers. Gentlemen: Having been nominated by your committee for a Pension of the above Society, I most earnestly solicit your Votes and kind interest. I was in the Trade about twenty-one years, leaving in 1891 through ill-health and have been unable to work in the Trade since. I am sorry to say I am a chronic invalid, suffering from asthma, bronchitis and gastritic, which prevents me from doing but little work and that of a very light nature, and, not being qualified for any other trade, find it rather hard to obtain a livelihood for myself and family. I am married, with four children, two dependent. I have now been out of the Trade for fourteen years, and, until last year, have never applied to the Society for assistance, and, as long as able to do so, contributed to the funds.

My last two situations were: eight years with the late Mr S. Barnett, 6 St George's Circus, Southwark, SE, and nine years with the late Mr Walter Knapp, 32 and 34 Church Street,

Edgware Road, who was my last employer. I subscribed to the Society twenty-seven years (1873 to 1900). My case is strongly recommended by a number of gentlemen. Being unable to personally canvas the Trade I shall esteem it a favour if Subscribers will kindly send on their votes, which will be gratefully acknowledged.

Trusting to meet with your kind support, I am, gentlemen, your obedient servant,

George Frank Gomm, 9 Percy Road, Kilburn, London NW[27]

For some reason, women had been consistently refused membership of the Benevolent Society, although there were many of them, and the number was increasing each year.

It was not until after the First World War, however, that a move was made to set up a National Union of Assistant Pawnbrokers, whose interests certainly merited proper representation. There were a great many of them, possibly 25,000 over the British Isles as a whole, and there was no difficulty about recruiting them. Advertisements provide interesting details of the labour market in pawnbroking before the First World War.

Wanted a Young Man, twelve to fifteen years' experience; one used to seaside trade preferred; single; to live in. Apply stating full particulars by letter to Pawnbroker, 'Pawnbrokers' Gazette' Office.

Wanted a respectable Young Man, about eight years' experience, for the Sale; assist at Pledge Counter when required; good references; specimen ticket; photo and salary. Live in. Apply Joseph Coleman Ltd, 9 Corn Market, Worcester.

Wanted a Willing Lad for the Shop to write tickets and book-up. Apply Mr Clears, 27 Goldhawk Road, Shepherd's Bush, w.

Wanted by Advertiser, single, aged 26, a re-engagement as Salesman, used to both Counters; well up in jewellery, clothing, etc.; good ticket writer; used to large outside show and busy trade; twelve years' experience; excellent references; disengaged; W.H.M., 8 Willow Bridge Street, Leicester.[28]

It is curious, given the number of new entrants to the trade each year, at least until the 1920s, that pawnbroking has produced

94

so little in the way of formal, organised instruction for its young men and women. It has always been reckoned that training had to be on the job and that there was no other effective way of gaining the necessary skill and experience. The weakness of this argument is that all purely in-service training, whether in pawnbroking or in any other occupation, can be no better than the person providing it. A first-class, progressive pawnbroker with a varied business might well be able to give a young person an excellent training which would stand him in good stead for the rest of his career, but a run-down, neglected business could offer only very limited opportunities indeed. It is no real answer to say that an ambitious person could always move from place to place to widen his knowledge. An enterprising employer would usually be disinclined to take on someone with poor previous experience. A well-planned, well-run course organised by an independent outside body, with the support of the trade, gives the average apprentice a better chance and helps to even out the difference between the good and the bad employer.

Nowadays most pawnbrokers, at least in London, give their assistants every opportunity and encouragement to undertake part-time study in gemmology and other branches of the jewellery business. But this is a recent development. Nothing similar existed before 1939, and one therefore notices with particular interest a large advertisement from Mr Arthur Tremayne of Holborn Circus in 1912, offering 'the only course of instruction that exists for pawnbrokers'. The course cost four pounds and for those students who completed it satisfactorily a diploma was granted. How many people took advantage of this opportunity we shall probably never know.

NOTES

1 At that time Clifton was one of Bristol's fashionable residential areas.
2 Conversation with the author, 3 December 1980.
3 Conversation with the author, 4 December 1980.
4 T. Layman and Sons, Ltd.
5 This would appear to indicate that pledges were not taken on every day of the week.
6 This machine was introduced in 1895. It was the only significant piece of mechanisation the pawnbroking trade has ever had. It worked on a pantograph principle, so that the operator's hand movements, as he wrote the ticket, were transferred to two other pens. The tickets, which were required by law, contained a good deal of detail and writing them out was a tedious business. One copy was for the customer, one for the office, and one for fixing to the goods.
7 Information provided on 3 December 1980.
8 Information provided on 11 September 1980.
9 *The Times*, 10 October 1961.
10 *The Times*, 28 January 1957.
11 On this, see Robert Roberts, *The Classic Slum*, 1971, pp. 11–12.
12 Ibid, p. 12.
13 *The Times*, 3 January 1917.
14 *The Times*, 5 January 1917.
15 *The Pawnbrokers' Gazette*, 22 March 1902.
16 It is reported in *The Pawnbrokers' Gazette*, 27 May 1905.
17 *The Pawnbrokers' Gazette*, 12 August 1905.
18 *The Pawnbrokers' Gazette*, 4 January 1902.
19 *The Pawnbrokers' Gazette*, 18 January 1902.
20 *The Pawnbrokers' Gazette*, 28 January 1905.
21 *The Pawnbrokers' Gazette*, 28 January 1905.
22 *The Pawnbrokers' Gazette*, 18 February 1905.
23 *The Pawnbrokers' Gazette*, 27 August 1910.
24 *The Pawnbrokers' Gazette*, 17 February 1912.
25 *The Pawnbrokers' Gazette*, 21 December 1912.
26 *The Pawnbrokers' Gazette*, 2 September 1905.
27 *The Pawnbrokers' Gazette*, 28 January 1905.
28 Examples taken from *The Pawnbrokers' Gazette*, 21 January 1905.

10 Sir John Swaish as Lord Mayor of Bristol.

11 The Council of the National Pawnbrokers' Association, early 1920s.
The President, Walter Bull, is in the front row, second from the left,
and the Honorary Secretary, F. K. Ohlson, is on his left.

12 Belfast Pawnbrokers' outing, 1930. At that time there were ninety
pawnbrokers' shops in Belfast, and consequently plenty of scope for
social activities.

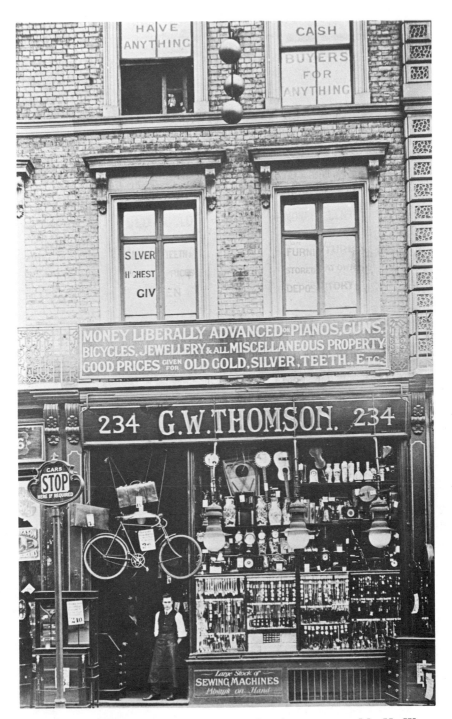

13 G. W. Thomson, 234 Praed Street, London, c. 1912. Mr H. W. Mobbs, the manager, then aged 24, is in the doorway.

14 The Board Room at the headquarters of the National Pawnbrokers'
Association, with painting of Walter Bull above the fireplace.

15 Interior of T. M. Sutton's shop, Victoria, c. 1939.

6

The Inter-war Years and the Great Depression

The world economic crisis of the Thirties was heralded by the Wall Street crash of 1929 and it was fully under way once the financial structure of Austria and Germany had collapsed during the summer of 1931. During 1932 and 1933 it developed into a severe and prolonged depression, which affected the whole of the Western world. In the early part of 1929 unemployment in Britain had been about 1,250,000. A year later it had risen to 1,750,000 and by the beginning of 1931 to 2,600,000. It reached its peak, 2,900,000 in September 1931, and it stayed at that level until November 1933, when it began to fall slowly. By the summer of 1937 the number of registered unemployed had gone down to 1,500,000.

Between 1930 and 1933 money wages fell, on the average, by about five per cent, but the fall in world prices caused their purchasing power to rise, so that in 1933 even the reduced money wages brought about eleven per cent more goods than the higher wage of 1929. The millions who had to suffer intermittent employment, as well as those who were actually unemployed, saw their purchasing power reduced; unemployment pay did not, at best, amount to more than a third of a man's regular earnings, and there was a stringent and much resented Family Means Test, which came into action when an unemployed person had been receiving what was known as 'standard benefit' – 'the dole' – under the Unemployment Insurance Scheme.

From an historical point of view, there are two ways of looking at this situation. One can say that, compared with someone who had no work in 1900, when there was no system of unemployment insurance in Britain at all, the unemployed man and his family were relatively well off in 1930. Or one can point out, with equal truth, that, as a result of much more general government provision since 1945, unemployed people are much better protected against hardship now than they were half a century earlier. It is also reasonable to point out that, if one allows for the rise in population, unemployment is running at about the same rate today as it was fifty years ago. But it exists in a different social and economic context.

In the Thirties, households where the breadwinner was unemployed operated on an economic cycle, in which the pawnshops played a vital role.

> In Liverpool two out of three unemployed families admit to having goods in pawn, and in some instances the whole economy of the home is so much dominated by the pawnshop that as soon as the clothes are bought through a clothing club, they go into the pawnshop and are never redeemed; and the clothing club thus becomes an even more uneconomical way of 'saving'. This process was described to us in Liverpool homes. In one, which was exceptionally well managed, the woman had had to pawn her engagement and wedding rings, and the watch given her on her twenty-first birthday by her husband, to meet the cost of an illness, and in others similar details were given. In no other place had pawning anything like such a hold as it evidently had in Liverpool.[1]

Against the economic background of the Twenties and Thirties one might well have expected the number of pawnshops to rise, or at least to hold their own, but in fact there was a marked decline. The figures for a selection of the major cities point the trend unmistakably. They refer to the number of pawnshops, not to the number of firms, and they are based on the street directories for the years in question. The total for 1980 is added to show how the decline has continued since the end of the Second World War.

	1900	1939	1980
Birmingham	328	128	none
Bristol	54	20	2
Cardiff	34	17[2]	2
Cork	21	18	1
Glasgow	125	78	15[3]

	1900	**1939**	**1980**
Leeds	127	65[4]	2
Manchester	285	160	6
Plymouth	28	20	none
Portsmouth	30	16	3

But one can get a great deal more information from street directories than mere statistics. It is interesting to see, for example, the kind of businesses that pawnbrokers had for their neighbours. Consider, for example, some groups of shops in the Scotswood Road, Newcastle. Who was on the left and the right-hand side of the pawnbroker?

In 1900 a typical pattern was:

203	McAllister, D.	innkeeper
209	Hyman, M.	pawnbroker
211	Browne, J. S.	fruiterer
415	River Plate Fresh Meat Co.	
417	Young & Co.	pawnbrokers
421	Kirkwood, J.	turner
	King, T.	joiner
674	Walker, J. W.	hairdresser
672	Davidson, J. P.	pawnbroker
670	Worthington, J. H.	grocer
496	Neve, T.	cart proprietor
492	Cohen, J.	pawnbroker
490	Wiggins, W.	blacksmith
142	Tomlinson, E., Mrs.	lodgings
140	Cash Trading Co.	pawnbrokers
136	Ferguson, R.	pig salesman

The pawnbroker was just as much a part of the local community as the grocer and the lodging-house keeper. And in working-class areas one had to go no more than a hundred yards, often much less, to find him.

Twenty years later, nothing had changed. The social mix had remained exactly the same.

99

32	Coffee, J.	general dealer
30	Spencer, J.	pawnbroker
26	Birkett, A.	butcher
80	Storey, S., Mrs.	fruiterer
78	Vilenski, M.	pawnbroker
76	Oakes, F.	shopkeeper

And that was how Scotswood Road was right up to its end in the 1950s, when it was officially designated a slum area and demolished from end to end. Its thirty-six pubs went at the same time, with their splendid names – 'The Hydraulic Crane', 'The Rifle', 'The Ordnance', 'The Forge Hammer', 'The Blast Furnace' – which reflected Armstrong's shipyard and armaments factory, which had brought the Scotswood Road into existence in the first place. In its heyday it may well have had the highest proportion of pawnbrokers to population in the British Isles, which is one kind of distinction, and there is no doubt that its inhabitants were ripe for rehousing. Even after the Second World War the houses were grossly over-crowded. 'Some had four families using one front door, others had three or four families using one tap and one toilet situated in the back yard.'[5]

During the Thirties conditions were hard in the Scotswood Road. Voluntary bodies gave what help they could, especially to the children, and the pawnshop was more important than ever. 'The police charity used to hand out boots and clogs. They would be given out one day, the next day the boots would be in pawn and the kids, if asked what happened to the boots, gave the stock reply – they were too tight and had been sent to the cobblers to be stretched.'[6]

Or one can take a careful look at the pawnbrokers listed in the directories, to see what evidence they provide for the often-heard assertion that a high proportion of pawnbrokers were Jewish. In this connection one thinks first, perhaps, of London and here, if the directories can be taken as a reliable guide, the popular belief has all the appearance of being nothing more than a myth. In the Post Office Directory for 1890, under the heading, 'Pawnbrokers and Silversmiths', there are 325 names, of which no more than fourteen sound in any way Jewish. In 1914 the total is 282, with only five possibly Jewish. Thom's Directory of Dublin lists forty-two pawnbrokers in the 1880 edition. Not one has a Jewish name.

Belfast, where pawnbroking was particularly reputed to be a Jewish occupation, had ninety-one firms in 1890. One, and only one, sounds as if the proprietor, Moses Finlay, might conceivably be Jewish, and even he could quite well have been a Presbyterian Scot with a biblically-minded father.

One can interest oneself, too, in the balance, at various dates, and in different towns and cities, between the big firms and the small ones. Using, for example, the *Edinburgh and Leith Post Office Directory*, in its 1919–20 edition, the pattern is as follows:

Equitable Loan Company of Scotland	13 branches
Hill Bros. Ltd.	14 branches
Hill, William	4 branches
Williamson, James and Sons	4 branches
and 32 other pawnbrokers, each with only	1 branch

By 1939, the proportion of big firms to small firms had changed very little, although the total had declined. The Equitable Loan Company was still active, although with only seven branches, instead of thirteen twenty years earlier. Hill Bros. had gone up from fourteen to sixteen, as a result of buying up one or two of their competitors. William Hill had disappeared altogether, Williamsons were down to two branches, and there were eighteen one-shop firms.

Behind the statistics and fleshing them out with a meaning that was not apparent at the time was a very significant historical fact. The people who were adults when the 1939–45 war broke out represented the last generation for whom the pawnshop was a normal way of life. Their children grew up under different circumstances, in a world where it was increasingly taken for granted that the State looked after those who were unable or who did not choose to look after themselves. Working-class families in the Thirties had much the same problems and much the same means of coping with them as their parents or grandparents, but to men and women with young children in the Fifties or Sixties the pre-war stories of privation and poverty came to sound like voices from another century. For these people, reared in the Welfare State, it does no harm to be reminded, in the words of those who were directly and personally concerned, how things were before the war turned British society upside down. Without these memories, the role the pawnbroker played at the time can never be properly understood.

The self-reliant society has largely disappeared and, to anyone who never knew it, it appears incredible and impossible.

We begin with a piece of autobiography from a man whose career in pawnbroking spanned forty-eight years, from the early Twenties to the late Sixties, Samuel Allen of Belfast. He came in when the trade was operating much as it had done for half a century, and he went out as the remaining Belfast pawnbrokers were being bombed out, burnt out and shot out by the IRA.

I started as an apprentice to the pawnbroking trade [he recalls][7] on the 22nd of August 1921. I was thirteen years and seven months of age. I remember the first Monday I started in Thomas G. Martin's shop at 5–7 Berlin Street, Shankill Road. He told me to stand and watch how to enter the articles for pledge in the Ledger Book. When I had watched for a while, Mr Martin told me to be ready to write in the Ledger. He called out to me, 'Hose, Shirt and Drawers'. I thought he said 'Old Shirt and Drawers', and I wrote that down in the book and on the Pledge Ticket. When he looked at the ticket and saw what I had written, he pushed me to one side and got the other wee lad to correct my mistake.

In those days they pledged life-sized photographs of husbands and wives, and a lot of hardware goods – pots, pans, steel fenders and black iron ones, with 'Home Sweet Home' on them, ash-pans, big iron mangles with wooden rollers, iron bed-ends with brass rods and knobs at the top, ruby vases and decanters, gramophones with the large horn.

On Mondays we took anything up to 700 pledges, but on Tuesdays they dropped down to 200–300. Friday and Saturday were our busy days, when the week's pledges were taken out. The hours were long, from 9 to 6.30 with an hour for lunch, Monday to Friday, Saturday 9 to 9. I started at 10s. a week and after the first year I had a 2s. 6d. rise. By the time I'd been 6 years with T. G. Martin I was getting £1 5s. Then I left him to go to work in a sale room for Joe Shaw, at £1 10s. a week. I stayed with him for about a year and then I was unemployed, with 10s. a week dole.

T. G. Martin advertised for an assistant, as the man he had was emigrating to America. I applied and he took me back. That was in about 1929, and I was with him until he retired in

1945. H. A. Lynn bought the business and kept me on as manager in charge, until I retired in 1969. When he took over he made a lot of changes. He got electric light installed in all the rooms upstairs and cleared out a lot of old goods.

I got a £1 rise in my first pay packet with him. He took stock in March 1945 and after that he gave me another £1 rise. When I left in 1969 my pay was £15 a week. The hours at that time were 9 to 6, and 6.30 on Saturday, and as years went on they were 9 to 5.30 and 6 on Saturday, with all day off on Wednesday. All the years I worked for T. G. Martin, the summer holiday was from Monday night to Saturday morning. When Lynn took over, he gave us from Saturday night until the following Monday.

On Monday mornings all along the counter were women with their pledges. T.G. would ask for 'a dry half one', meaning snuff. He would take a pinch between his thumb and fore-finger and say, 'Up your nose, down to your toes, so here goes.'

After the First World War, the pawnshops were flooded with German cut-throat razors. All kinds of strange things were pawned in those days. One old fellow used to pawn his false teeth for half a crown, and a chap by the name of John Bingham made a violin from a Sunlight Soap box and used to pledge it for 5s. When he came in to pledge or redeem it, he always gave the old ladies in the shop a few tunes on it. Orange and black sashes were also pawned. The orange sashes were redeemed for the month of July and the black ones for August. Flutes and fifes were sold at this time of the year. Transistor radios, record-players, tape recorders and good watches are all they take in now.

When I look back, it makes me wonder why I stayed in pawn-broking so long. I know many young fellows, and older men, who were in the business and left for better places of employ-ment.

Joseph Nugent spent more than forty years as a pawnbroker's assistant in Belfast, retiring in the early Seventies. He served his apprenticeship at McKeown's shop in Great Patrick Street, which was on the edge of the city's 'Little Italy' area, inhabited by the poorer members of the Italian community in Belfast. They were interesting people, who used the pawnshops in their own special way.

> They were [Mr Nugent remembers], mostly engaged in making and selling ice cream from their small carts with a compartment for the freezer and another for the tins of wafers. When winter came they worked at terrazzo flooring and one or two made alabaster statues which they sold to the shops or round the doors. When there was no work the freezer and sometimes the cart itself found its way round to McKeown's pawn in Great Patrick Street, where there was a large storage space, and stayed there till Easter.[8]

A storage charge was allowed by law on bulky articles, such as trunks, large suitcases, kitchen fenders and, of course, ice cream carts. The pawner was asked to pay a fixed charge, usually a shilling in the pound per month, and this was written on the ticket.

Some of the Belfast pawnbrokers had a reputation for particular kinds of knowledge and expertise.

> McKeown's [says Joseph Nugent] specialised in good jewellery, silver plate and binoculars and old violins and had built up a good retail sale trade in these articles. Rogers in Union Street also had a good trade in jewellery but his speciality was tools for all trades. The last Edmund Murray succeeded to this business and carried it on to his death. Bob Adgey on Peter's Hill was an authority on guns and ammunition and was himself a crack shot, having won prizes at Bisley. He was Col. Crawford's right hand man in the arming of the Ulster Volunteers in 1912 and published a book on the subject. In the King Street area was another pawn office with storage space and going back to Marquis Street and the famous Lord Lurgan of 'Master McGrath' fame is supposed to have stored his carriage and pair there after a bad night at the cards.

After mixing with them for forty years, Mr Nugent came to the conclusion that pawnbrokers were by no means a bad lot. 'The majority of the men I knew in the trade,' he reflected, 'were hardworking reputable businessmen, shrewd judges in the stock and property market. You had of course the odd foxy one who wasn't above exploiting the people by overcharging interest, who was the exception rather than the rule.'

Ernest Hush, of Middlesbrough, ran his own pawnshops during the depression of the Thirties and finally retired from the business in 1966. In the early years many of his customers were illiterate and asked Mr Hush to write letters for them. 'I have even,' he says, 'made a few wills.'[9] When he thinks back to those days, what particularly saddened him was 'the realisation of knowing that people had no, repeat *no* money in their possession on Monday morning. They came to pawn their possessions at 7 a.m. (at one period) to enable them to buy food for breakfast. I came to recognise and understand the submerged state of always being hard up and accepting living from hand to mouth as a normal way of life. Our business sometimes came to a standstill because people had nothing left to pawn.'

One wonders what people would have done in those days if there had been no pawnshops. When the question was put to them, pawnbrokers who were active during the Twenties and Thirties gave a variety of answers. One can most usefully list them under the name of the town concerned.

Liverpool – 'Some people would have gone hungry. There were moneylenders, but the interest they charged was very high. People did borrow from each other from week to week.'[10]

Liverpool – 'The majority of them would have suffered in silence. The rest would probably have resorted to thieving and mugging.'[11]

Mexborough – 'The only alternative to the pawnshop was the "parish" payment, where people had to suffer a degrading means test before any cash, however little, was offered.'[12]

Newcastle upon Tyne – 'They would have had to go to moneylenders, beg, or go to the Board of Guardians, or to Poor Relief. This was a very degrading business. Many a wedding ring and small article of sentimental value would have been pawned first.'[13]

Croydon – 'I am afraid many would have gone without food. In extreme circumstances, you got vouchers from the council for coal and groceries. You got these at the Co-op.'[14]

It is certainly possible that the pawnbroker stood between many poor people and crime during these harsh years. From force of circumstances and perhaps from temperament as well, he was a strange cross between the hard businessman and the friend in need. To construct anything like a stereotype of the pawnbroker between the wars would be both difficult and misleading – pawnbrokers, like the members of every other occupation, are individuals – but it is interesting to see what kind of men these pawnbrokers seemed to be to the people who worked with them week by week. Did they run to type? Were they conditioned to any extent by the social conditions of their time? These four profiles are offered mainly to stimulate interest and enquiry.

Charles Smith, of Liverpool – 'He was a devoted Catholic, very generous to his church. During business hours he wore a cap, but when he left for home it was always in a bowler hat. He very rarely lost his temper and was a very trusting man. He was well-known and much liked in the district. His staff always received a Christmas box each year.'[15]

Sammy Jacobs, of Newport, South Wales – 'He came from a well-known and respected Jewish family. He was a good man to the people of Pill [the dock area of Newport] and especially to the Catholics. He used to help them with the clothes they needed for their Corpus Christi procession.'[16]

Harold George Rendle, of Plymouth – 'He was a tall, lean man, balding and with a small moustache. He was always immaculately dressed. In the summer he discarded his jacket and worked in his waistcoat. From his waistcoat there always dangled an 18 carat gold Albert. At one end was a solid gold Benson or Waltham watch and on the other a gold sovereign case. The ensemble was rounded off with a diamond tie pin and diamond signet ring. As an employer he was strictly business and totally conservative. He took a great interest in local affairs and was a member of the Conservative Club, but he never got involved in politics as such. He regularly visited the Noah's Ark public house, which was a Men Only establishment. He was very strict at only valuing a pledge for its business worth.'[17]

J. B. H. Baker, of Bristol – 'He was a very strict, honest, straightforward man, but very tight with money. If I went to ask him for a rise, he'd say, "Oh, yes. I'll give you a rise on Friday when I pay you." His limit for a rise was sixpence a week.

And yet, if he was going home on the tram – he always did this on a Saturday, instead of riding his pushbike – and saw one of his customers on the tram, he'd say to the conductor, "Look, that lady there. Here's her fare." He used to live at Redcliffe Lodge, Filton. He called his house Redcliffe Lodge after the Masons. He belonged to the Masons.'[18]

Different people will, of course, produce different, often very different portraits of the same person. The politician as described on his electioneering leaflet may be almost unrecognisable to his wife and it is not unknown for the newspaper obituary of an eminent person to come as a considerable surprise to his friends. But no trade or profession can be better than the average level of its members, and for this reason the historian has a duty to collect and analyse whatever clues he can find to the qualities and personalities of the people earning a living by that occupation at different periods. It is, in any case, an agreeable and stimulating activity. All history is primarily about people, not about treaties, Acts of Parliament and legal decisions.

One of the most remarkable people ever to have been involved in the pawnbroking trade was Walter Bull, who died in 1927 in his 87th year. Mr Bull was the Association's President from 1913 to 1925. He was largely responsible for the decision to build Lombard House in the City of London as the Association's headquarters. It was opened in 1925, the total cost of £13,494 16s. 6d. having been met by donations.

The site had been generously donated to the Association by Mr Bull. The opening ceremony, *The Pawnbrokers' Gazette* reported,[19] was:

> One of the most enthusiastic gatherings ever held in the history of the pawnbroking trade, the only other function that can be compared with it being the celebrations in connection with the passing of the 1872 and the 1922 Acts. The first thing that brought forth ardent applause was the reading of the list of donations from various associations and towns. But the real enthusiasm was made manifest when Mr Walter Bull stepped forward to unlock the doors of the Council Room and that and subsequent events during the afternoon proved it was his day of triumph. Mr Bull, who was unfortunately not in the best of health, was obviously affected by his hearty welcome and there

must have been few present who did not feel moved during the late President's simple opening oration. Mr Bull's speech was a message of hope and encouragement for the future of the trade and he paid tribute to those who by their generosity had enabled the building to be erected. Mr Sidney Smith received the Home on behalf of the trade as a sacred trust to be carried on for the benefit of the members of the National Association and the welfare and advancement of the trade.

At the luncheon which followed the opening:

Mr Bull, in a stirring speech, maintained it was the first rung in the ladder to higher and greater things for the trade, and he appealed to the younger members to take up the work where he and others must, of necessity, leave off, by entering into public life and taking up greater responsibilities for the betterment of their calling, and of the community generally. Alderman Bowes, the doyen of the Manchester Corporation, spoke to like effect and said Mr Bull's life and work was an example to them all. Much food for thought may be found in the other speeches, all of which we heartily commend to our readers. Lombard House now stands as a symbol of unity and good purpose in the trade and as an everlasting memorial to the one who gave of his best to his fellow men and it is the duty of every member of the ancient Trade of Pawnbroking to see that the standard of honour and good work is never lowered.

When Mr Bull died an obituary reported:

He was also an outstanding figure in the civic life of the City of London. His funeral was attended by Pawnbrokers from all over the country, while a memorial service in the City was attended by the Lord Mayor and Sheriffs in state, as well as by representatives of various institutions with which he was connected in business and municipal life. It was the general feeling of members of the Association that something in the nature of a tablet should be set up in Lombard House to his memory, as it was to his foresight and generosity a headquarters for the Pawnbroking Trade was made possible. When the matter was broached at the annual Council Meeting, in May, 1927, it at once met with a sympathetic response. It was decided the memorial should take the form of a small bronze plaque. The

Executive Officers drew up suitable wording, which was approved by the Council. The tablet was subsequently fixed to the wall of the Council Chamber.[20]

Mr Bull had also, in 1914, presented the National Association with its Presidential Badge.

> The Presidential Badge, presented to the National Association by Mr Bull, in 1914, on his election to that high office, is made in massive 18-carat gold, trefoil in shape. The centre medallion is occupied by the figure of the Pawnbrokers' Patron Saint, Saint Nicholas, raised and chased in bold relief. He is robed in his canonical vestments crowned with the mitre, holding the Gospel in his left hand, on which are placed the three golden balls or bags of gold. His right hand grasps the crozier or pastoral staff, at his feet is the Association's motto in a ribbon of blue-enamel, '*Unitate Fortior*'. The figure is surrounded by a wreath of the National floral emblems, the Rose, Shamrock and Thistle, richly chased in relief. The three bosses contain respectively the Rose, the Shamrock and the Thistle, artistically enamelled in natural colours.[21]

To what extent the people nominated for election to the Council of the National Pawnbrokers' Association have been typical of its membership is not easy to judge. They may well be more energetic and more successful than the average, but they can hardly be a breed apart. Here, at any rate, are summaries of the biographies of the twelve candidates who were submitted to the Association's Triennial Meeting in 1925. They are likely to be as representative of the membership of the Association at that date as any other form of sampling which could have been chosen.

Mr Sam Robertshaw Ackroyd – Son of an Honorary Secretary of the Bradford Pawnbrokers' Association, he was educated at the local higher grade school and entered his father's business. 'He is a man of modesty, so far as concerns the limelight, but a remarkably skilful worker in the secretarial duties.' Member of the Council of the Bradford Chamber of Trade for five years. His interests include motor-cycling and angling.

Mr Joseph Clarkson – Apprenticed to the trade in Liverpool and appointed as manager at the age of nineteen. Bought his own business in Blackburn. On the death of his previous employer and of his legatees he purchased nine of his shops. A Conservative and a churchman.

Mr Robert Currie (Sr.) – Born in Scotland, he settled in Manchester at the age of thirteen and gained experience in the Scotch travelling drapery trade. He went over to the pawnbroking trade at the age of nineteen, his father having said, 'It's a gran' safe trade, ye see ye aye hold the one thing for the other.' Two years later he opened his own business, and later acquired many other shops. 'He brims over with good fellowship and is as breezy as he is rosy and merry and bright.' Has five sons and a son-in-law in the trade. Past President of the Manchester Pawnbrokers' Bowling Club.

Mr John Dickenson Eaton – Started in the trade at the bottom at the age of sixteen and at twenty-four was taken into partnership with his father. Now has five shops, two in Sheffield, one in Rotherham and one in Ilkeston. 'Mr Eaton in everything that concerns the Trade is, and has been, most zealous.' Personally, 'he is a man of very kindly disposition, thoughtful, and considerate to his employees'.

Mr Lewin P. Samuel – Started in the clothing trade and in 1888 acquired, in partnership with his father, a pawnbroking business in Birmingham. 'There is no more popular man in the Pawnbroking Trade in the Midlands. His energy, genial bearing and readiness at all times to give either advice or personal help to his fellow Pawnbrokers have won for him hearty goodwill throughout the district.' One of the originators of the Birmingham and District Pawnbrokers' Benevolent Association; a Director of James Collins Ltd.; Director of the Scala, Ltd.; and Managing Director of the Futurist.

Mr Henry Smetham – Born in Bristol, he entered the trade at the age of fifteen, in Bath. Trade defence has been a lifelong effort with him. He has 'literary propensities', and is a strong supporter of National Trade Unity. He has been a supporter of the National Pawnbrokers' Association since its inception. His public offices include libraries and museums, archaeology and philosophy. Member of the Dickens' Fellowship. His leisure activities include bowls.

Alderman Sir John Swaish, KBE, JP, DL – 'A capable and skilful business career has been supplemented by active and valued
service in civil rights, as well as by unstinted labours in the
spheres of both religious and political advancement.' Has served
for thirty-five years on Bristol City Council. In 1913 was Lord
Mayor of Bristol, and served for a second term. Later became
Chairman of the local Tribunal. Chairman of the Public Works
Committee. Chairman of the Watch Committee. Chairman of
the Colston Hall Management and the Town Planning Committee. 'He combines a far-sighted and logical power of discussing public affairs with a genial and kindly nature, winning
the friendship and goodwill even of political opponents. He is
a most capable and logical speaker.' A Deacon of Broadmead
Baptist Chapel. For twenty years Superintendent of the Sunday
School (one of the largest in the West Country).

Mr C. E. Sykes – Born in Leeds, the son of a pawnbroker, he
entered the trade at the age of thirteen with another pawnbroker, and then assisted his father. On his father's death he
and his mother carried on the business. Formerly a member of
the cricket team of the Leeds Assistants' Association. 'He has a
most sympathetic feeling for the assistants in the Trade.'
Member of the Council of the Leeds Chamber of Trades. Member of the Committee of the Leeds Credit Retailers' Association.
Vice-President of the Halton and District Institute.

Mr John Whiting – Born in Nottingham, the son of a box manufacturer, he was educated at Nottingham High School and
apprenticed to a pawnbroker for eight years before he started on
his own account. He now has six businesses. 'With his commit-
ments he has no inclination to engage in public work.' Interested in elementary education, he is Chairman of the Board of
four schools at Sneinton. A non-smoker and life-long abstainer.
His principal hobby is gardening.

Mr Emile Windsor – Born near Crewe, where his father carried
on a large grocery and provisions concern in the vicinity of an
iron and steel works. Attended the National Church School at
Crewe and gained a three-year scholarship. Member of Christ
Church choir. Obtained solo treble appointment at Torquay
Cathedral. The grocery business closed following the shut-down

of the iron and steel works and the family moved to Accrington, where he helped a lady pawnbroker and became manager 'at the earliest age'. He continued his musical studies. The family moved to Bolton and he found another job as assistant in a pawnbroker's shop, later becoming manager before being taken into partnership. Now he is the sole owner of the business.

Mr John Waterston – Born in Perth, the son of a pawnbroker who managed the Perth Loan Company. His father moved to Glasgow and he began his apprenticeship there. Now has two shops in Glasgow and is connected with a number of influential business undertakings in the city. Extremely popular with all ranks. Thoroughly familiar with the pawnbroking law.

Mr Patrick Gorman – For many years he was manager of the Central Pawn Office in Dublin, before acquiring his own business. 'Owing to his own modesty', not much else is known about him.[22]

A first comment on this most interesting catalogue might be: 'They could easily be bank managers, instead of pawnbrokers,' and the two types do indeed overlap to a remarkable extent. A certain breeziness, clubbability, and willingness to involve oneself in non-controversial social activities is a recipe for success in both callings.

There is a tendency, however, for the people who find their way on to governing bodies to be reasonably satisfied with life and to have most of their career behind them and for these reasons to hope that things will continue to go on much as they have in the past. A study of the files of *The Pawnbrokers' Gazette* for the Twenties and Thirties, however, reveals considerable and occasionally outspoken awareness that the trade was declining and that radical changes were necessary if it was to have any future.

Year by year, the January reports from around the country were almost uniformly gloomy, even before the great depression really got under way. Here are three assessments of the situation as it appeared in 1928.[23]

The first comes from Kent:

We regret that the trade of the entire district has been bad. Every pawnbroker finds his soft goods largely unsaleable and, of course, jewellery is a dead letter. His expenses are practically double their pre-war level; his profits largely remain stationary. The canker of unemployment leaves people engaged in all the competitive occupations in a bad situation . . . There has also arisen a tremendous growth of the hire purchase (or 'tally') system. The 'so much down, and so much a week as long as you live' system.

The second is from Plymouth:

Trading conditions in the West of England have not shown any improvement over those of the previous years and Pawnbroking does not come back or increase, in addition to which the ever present difficulty of handling women's attire, to be at all remunerative, is more pronounced than ever. The scanty and flimsy goods so much in vogue and so frequently changing in fashion, render them of little value after twelve months on the shelf. Men's clothing is different and there is always a ready sale for garments in good condition.

And the third relates to Glasgow:

The civil authorities have for some time past been devoting attention to the housing question and huge sums are being expended in providing new houses on the outskirts of the city, to which are being removed dispossessed families from older and congested districts. Such transference of the population is having a serious effect on Pawnbrokers in the latter districts and they are in the unhappy position of seeing their customers going away and their businesses dwindling without being able in any way to help themselves. There are no premises available for Pawnbrokers in the new suburbs and while offices near the housing schemes are doing increased business, this is no help to the others in the condemned property.

There was no report as such from London, but the *Gazette* was able to quote an article in the *Daily Mail*, based on an interview with 'the Secretary of one of the largest firms of Pawnbrokers in London'. This spokesman for the Trade found a different reason for pawnbrokers' troubles. 'In the main,' he felt, 'there is much less pawning in London than a few years ago. In the days after the war a large number of our customers were young married people, but now the numbers of this class on our books have been going down considerably. Young Londoners appear to be growing thriftier. They are earning more money than they used to and they are managing to live within their incomes.'[24]

It will be noticed that all these correspondents and experts attribute the poor state of trade to a range of external factors, not to any failings on the part of pawnbrokers themselves. It was all the fault of unemployment, the hire purchase system, frequent changes in fashion, slum clearance, a new determination to live within one's income – every pundit had his own explanation.

But the centre of the problem undoubtedly lay elsewhere. It was pungently and brutally defined in a letter written by a pawnbroker soon after the outbreak of the Second World War.

> Fundamentally and psychologically, Pawnbrokers are too conservative to make progress; their minds are glued to the operations of their ancestors, who produced the Parliamentary Act, and from that date (1872) the mind of the Trade (excepting such rebels as the present writer) stopped functioning.[25]

Much the same point was made in one of the entries to a competition organised in 1939 to try to discover the reasons for the decline of pawnbroking.

> The decline of pawnbroking [wrote F.S.B. of Chester] is no doubt due to the present generation being better educated and having a finer sense of money values than their parents had. Pledging to their parents was a part of their daily life, but not so to the children. To enter a Pawnbroker's shop is about the last thing they will do. Therefore, in my opinion, that class of pawner can no longer be depended upon to provide the bulk of the Pawnbroker's business. The Pawnbroker must go all out for the better-class people, who no doubt would greatly appreciate a loan if they knew how to go about it. Therefore to all Pawnbrokers I say Advertise! How many Pawnbrokers do advertise? Practically none. Let these people know that you would consider it a pleasure to advance them some ready cash on their valuables. If necessary, tell them that you will do the business by appointment.[26]

Other suggestions abounded, but few of them dug very deep. Pawnbrokers should remove the dust of ages from their shops and make them cleaner, brighter and more appealing; interests rates should be increased; service should be speeded up. A Hull pawn-broker even suggested that the root of the trouble was the three balls sign itself. He was, he said, ashamed of it. 'The Sign of the Three Brass Balls is one that has received more notice from the Press and public than any other sign I know, scathing and unjust remarks, all kinds of songs and vulgarity have been written and wound round them until it seems to me the sign has brought ridicule and contempt on the Trade itself.'[27]

Subsequent research revealed that tradition had already been defied to a limited extent.[28] Fox's, of Bootle, had combined the three brass balls with the Isle of Man sign – a change which might have made good sense in Douglas, but seemed to have little to commend it in Bootle. Hyde's, of Crown Street, Liverpool, were daringly displaying three *silver* balls; and several shops, whether from ignorance or design, were hanging the sign the wrong way up.

And all the time Parliament and the courts were busy closing a loophole here, tying in a loose end there. With good reason pawn-brokers claimed that they were the most controlled of all the trades and professions. Lawyers certainly had reason to be grateful that pawnbroking existed.[29]

In 1924 there was the Pawning Industrial Tools Bill, to prevent a man pawning tools which belonged not to him but to his em-ployer. In 1932 there was a clause in the Children's Bill, which made it illegal for pawnbrokers to deal with children under the age of sixteen, a change that was bitterly resisted by the National Pawnbrokers' Association, mainly on the somewhat melodramatic grounds that it would 'play into the hands of small secret money-lenders who blackmailed women'. On a slightly lower level there was, from the point of view of the legal profession, a most agreeable series of court cases involving people who made use of pawnbrokers for one fraudulent purpose or another. The reports of some of these make excellent reading and it is a pity they are not more easily available. One case, of great importance to the trade, involved a firm of jewellers, two London pawnbrokers, and an ingenious swindler named Lewis Waller.[30]

Waller's technique was simple. He visited London Jewellers Ltd. and obtained from them a number of items of jewellery on approval, saying that he was in a position to sell them to actresses. What in fact he did was to hand them straight away to three female accom-plices, who then pawned them, in their own names, with Mr

Thomas Miller Sutton of Victoria Street or Messrs Robertson's of Edgware Road. London Jewellers demanded from the pawnbrokers either the return of the items of jewellery or their value. Alternatively, they claimed damages for wrongful conversion of the articles. It was admitted that in taking the articles in pledge the pawnbrokers acted in good faith. It was plain that they knew nothing of Waller and believed they were trading solely with the women who handed them the goods. These actions were regarded as test cases and the decision would affect a considerable number of other pawnbrokers with whom Waller had dealt, through his agents, with property similarly obtained. Mr Justice Swift found for the plaintiffs, London Jewellers but, to the great relief of the pawnbrokers and their Association, the verdict was reversed on appeal.

Fighting an action like this was an expensive business and reinforced the pawnbrokers' belief that they were in a hazardous occupation for which they did not receive adequate recognition or compensation. It is therefore a pleasure to be able to record that one of the two defendants in the Waller case, Mr Thomas Miller Sutton, did not die a poor man. The business he founded near Victoria Station[31] became known as 'the Harrods among pawnbrokers', and many of the British and Continental aristocracy and gentry were among his customers. A Yorkshireman, he died in 1934, leaving a fortune of $£1\frac{1}{4}$ million, which was distinctly above average for pawnbrokers at that time. Under the terms of his will, each member of the staff received a year's wages and the taxi-man who took him to and from work each day, a 3d. fare, was given the money to buy himself two new taxis. Among his many other talents, Thomas Miller Sutton, so it is said, could tell how many carats a gold object was merely by feeling it.

Mr Sutton maintained a 'favourite customers' book, which contained the names and addresses of his more important and distinguished clients. Many of them were titled and many lived abroad. A glance through its pages reveals such elegant addresses as the Piccadilly Hotel, the Army and Navy Club, Upper Cheyne Walk, Boulevard Haussmann, Buckingham Palace Road, St John's Wood, Biarritz, Alexandria and Petrograd. At Sutton's one was indeed a very long way from the Scotswood Road and the associations with poverty and misery which characterised that end of the trade. Before the 1939–45 war, recalled Mr John Sharp, who spent the whole fifty years of his working life with Sutton's, 'We had twenty tiaras at any one time,' adding, 'I haven't seen one for years.'

To obtain business, Sutton's had three Continental agents working for them before the outbreak of war in 1939 put an end to this system for ever. One agent, Mr Richardson, was based in Cannes, one, Mr Delfau, in Paris, and one, Messrs Goldschmidt and Weisman, in Berlin. They were given a percentage commission for getting the business and for bringing the goods to London for sale or for pledging. Their couriers came to London once a fortnight, travelling overnight to and from Victoria, and the articles they brought accounted for half Sutton's business before 1939. They brought over their precious freight in the numerous chamois leather pockets of specially made waistcoats and took back the proceeds in large denomination bank notes, safely packed away in a cloth belt worn under the shirt.

Sutton's got the French business mainly because the pawning process in France was slow and cumbersome. The police required identity documents, proof of ownership and receipts before a transaction could be cleared. Consequently, clients needing money quickly preferred to deal with Sutton's, via Messrs Delfau and Richardson.[32]

John Sharp, who began work at Sutton's as a shop-boy, sleeping under the counter, eventually became manager of the business and has had a wide range of duties in his time with the firm. From 1932 to 1935, when the stock contained some particularly valuable items, there was a guard dog on the premises. Mr Sharp bought him from Battersea Dogs' Home. He was exceptionally ferocious and he was in Mr Sharp's personal charge.

NOTES

1 John Stevenson, *Social Conditions in Britain Between the Wars*, 1977, page 275, quoting a report by the Pilgrim Trust.
2 The total is for 1937, the nearest available date.
3 This figure includes one old-established firm (1830), Robert Biggar Ltd, whose directory entry is marked 'Business strictly private. Postal transactions by return.'
4 The total is for 1940. No directory was issued in 1939.
5 On life in the Scotswood Road, see Thomas Callaghan, *A Lang Way to the Pa'shop*, c.1979, and Arthur Stabler, 'Ganning along the Scotswood Road: a social history of the Scotswood community from 1847', paper read at the meeting of the British Association, Lancaster, 1976. Typescript in Newcastle Central Library, p. 21. Demolition began in 1953.
6 Stabler, op. cit., p. 17.
7 Letter to the author, 30 November 1980.
8 Reminiscence sent to the author, 17 December 1980.
9 Letter to the author, 1 January 1981.
10 Francis Hutchinson, 31 December 1980.
11 C. Grummant, 20 December 1980.
12 C. R. Pocklington, 13 January 1981.
13 Thomas D. Rodham, 6 January 1981.
14 S. A. Greenhead, 28 January 1981.
15 Francis Hutchinson, 31 December 1980.
16 Dick Godwin of Brecon, 3 December 1980.
17 V. R. Gray, 12 January 1981.
18 Charles Allsopp, 4 December 1980.
19 31 October 1925.
20 National Pawnbrokers' Association of Great Britain and Ireland: *Official Souvenir of the Eleventh Triennial Meeting* at Bristol, 1928, p. 32. This publication contains a useful appendix, 'Pawnbrokers in Public Life', with a long list of pawnbrokers who were or had been MPs, Lord Mayors, Mayors and JPs.
21 *Official Souvenir of the Eleventh Triennial Meeting*, p. 34.
22 *The Pawnbrokers' Gazette*, 9 May 1925.
23 *The Pawnbrokers' Gazette*, 5 January 1929.
24 *The Pawnbrokers' Gazette*, 5 January 1929.
25 *The Pawnbrokers' Gazette*, 17 February 1940.
26 *The Pawnbrokers' Gazette*, 12 August 1939.
27 *The Pawnbrokers' Gazette*, 9 January 1926. The New York pawnbrokers did precisely this forty years later, when *The Times* (25 June 1964) reported that they had replaced the three balls by three interconnecting spirals, 'thereby raising the dignity of the business'.
28 *The Pawnbrokers' Gazette*, 4 May 1940.

29 The complexities of pawnbroking law and the fine variety of cases which arose from it are excellently illustrated in Charles L. Attenborough's book, *The Law Affecting Pawnbroking*, 1905.
30 The case was fully reported in *The Times*, 20 January 1934.
31 For some years it has been owned by Mappin and Webb.
32 On this, see an article by John Sharp in *News and Views*, the house journal of Mappin and Webb, Vol. 27, No. 1, Autumn 1979.

7

Pawnbroking in the Age of
Social Security and the Welfare State

The history of pawnbroking, as described in the previous chapters of this book, could be summarised roughly as follows. It began in medieval Europe by lending money to the rich and powerful, it expanded enormously during the eighteenth and nineteenth centuries by providing a means by which the urban poor could manage to keep their heads above water, and it began to decline from the 1930s onwards, as the State found itself under increasing pressure to take the basic care of the poor into its own charge and as the British working class began to enjoy a level of prosperity, comfort and security which would have seemed inconceivable before 1939.

During the 1940s and 1950s, when what might be called the pawning classes either lost the habit of pawning or never acquired it, pawnbrokers closed down by the hundred, either because they could find more profitable things to do or because sons and daughters had no wish to carry on the family business. As pawnbroking became concentrated into fewer and fewer hands, those who had stayed the course managed to make a respectable and sometimes a very good living by attracting customers who came from greater and greater distances and who represented a much wider social cross-section than before the war. Today one can see the beginnings of a very different kind of trade and the emergence of a new type of pawnbroker. The trade, not for the first time, has shown itself to be remarkably adaptable to new conditions and the 1980s are likely to see some most interesting developments, as pawnbroking shakes itself free from the old association with poverty and returns to something closer to its medieval beginnings, lending money to people who are quite well blessed with this world's goods already.

Against the background of this general thesis, the years since 1945 can and probably should be regarded not so much as a period of slow death for pawnbroking, which is how most observers inside and outside the trade have seen it, but as a necessary phase of clearing the ground in readiness for a new movement forward. The old-style pawnbroking has almost reached its end, after playing an important part in British society for many generations; its successor is not yet recognised for what it is, and the last few pages of this book will be devoted to an attempt to identify it and to describe some of its characteristics, as they have so far revealed themselves.

There is no more dramatic way of documenting the decay and disappearance of pawnbroking as our grandparents knew it than by examining a list of the Pawnbrokers' Protection Societies which were federated with the National Pawnbrokers' Association of Great Britain and Ireland at twenty-year intervals from the beginning of this century, with the number of members in each Society for the given dates.[1] Only those Societies for which there are records for all five dates are listed below.

Society	1900	1920	1940	1960	1980
Metropolitan	506	523	410	170	49
Liverpool, Birkenhead & District	175	162	172	76	16
Manchester, Salford & District	167	173	159	59	5
Birmingham & District	128	110	107	13	3
Glasgow	96	123	180	136[2]	25
Sheffield, Rotherham & District	89	112	78	31	1
Leeds	55	70	48	7	2
North Staffordshire	49	54	40	5	0
Bolton & District	40	45	29	2	0
Belfast	38	40	45	32[3]	6
Newcastle, Gateshead & District	33	41	44	26	4
Middlesbrough, Stockton & District	25	13	12	10	1
Nottingham & District	24	32	32	17	2
Leicester & Leicestershire	24	21	19	9	1

Society	1900	1920	1940	1960	1980
Bristol & District	21	31	30	14	2
Portsmouth, Southsea & Landport	18	20	13	13	4

To those who take a conservative view of the pawnbroking trade and its potential, these are depressing figures. They fully support both the title and theme of an article which appeared in *The Times* in 1957, 'Vanishing Pawnbrokers: Only the Fittest Survive in the Welfare State'.[4] There had been an equally gloomy and self-assured article seven years earlier.[5] This is how the situation appeared to its author.

'A gentleman,' said Mr Smangle to Mr Pickwick, 'must expect reverses.' In the annual reports of Customs and Excise the pawnbroker may see how poignantly his expectations have been fulfilled. The road has led downhill at least since 1931–2, when in England and Wales there flourished 3,001 pawnbrokers and in Scotland 383. In 1935–6 there were 2,643 and 338; in 1943–4 1,773 and 265; and in 1948–9, 1,507 and 219. This year, it is thought, will bring another reduction.

The blight has struck impartially north and south, and there appears to have been an equal mortality of the flamboyant golden balls that illuminated drab districts and the discreet pilules that whispered of succour in west ends.

Social students have welcomed it all as a token of a rare deep economic transformation, an exegesis that is supported by a fall in the number of moneylenders from 3,519 in 1931–2 to 1,588 in 1948–9. But regular work and goods, it is believed, have been assisted by the growth of hire purchase.

Nevertheless, a common experience used to be that business sharpened not in severe depressions, but in fairly good times when a pawner, although temporarily hard up, could be sure of being able to redeem her napery and trinkets at the week's or month's end.

Before the war it was not rare for a poor family's better clothes to go in on Monday and come out for Sunday's special occasions; and even now some of the most esteemed clients are said to be members of the salaried class, who pawn in anticipation of a monthly cheque. In really evil days the pawner had no intention (or perhaps hope) of redeeming.

A factor in the trade's decline may well be the pawnbroker's sense that there are more profitable things to do. He is governed by the strict rod of the Pawnbrokers Acts, which order his benevolences in detail. Below £10 (where the rules differ), in addition to the halfpence for the pawn ticket or 1d. over 10s., he can levy interest of ½d. per month on every 2s. where the loan is less than 40s., and on every 2s. 6d. where the loan exceeds 40s. Since 1922 a concession has allowed him to add an extra ½d. for every 5s. lent. The interest can be calculated to look large, but as low profits close his business the broker at last finds an answer to his critics.

The analysis is not unfair, but throughout the article one senses that the writer is shedding few tears on the pawnbroker's behalf. 'The trade,' he takes trouble to say, 'has usually had fewer friends than clients.'

A similarly superior, if not actually hostile note, is struck by the writer of the 1957 article. 'Only the other day,' he observes, 'news came out of Burton-on-Trent that the town's last surviving pawnbroking business had closed for good, and we may guess that nobody particularly mourned its passing. It has become a familiar story. For four decades at least, and especially during the last ten years, the old Lombard signs of the three brass balls have been dropping from their brackets as though they were deciduous things blasted by some withering storm.'

He is impressed by the fact that in 1949 1,507 pawnbroking licences were issued by the Customs and Excise in England and Wales and 219 in Scotland, compared with 3,001 and 383 in 1931–2, and he goes on to say that factors affecting the fall include 'full employment, good wages, a comprehensive Welfare State, hire-purchase, and better schooling'. But this, he believes, is not the whole story. Pawnbroking was always 'very much a dynastic occupation', and 'sons had risen above the trade'. Working-class people had been rehoused in areas where there were no pawnshops. Pawnbrokers with a retail side to their business in addition to pawnbroking had decided to concentrate on that, especially where the other line was jewellery, because it brought them a higher rate of profit. Most important of all, the character and quality of the trade had undergone a fundamental change. Pawnbrokers were taking in many fewer pledges than previously, but of much greater value. The pawnbroker therefore gets his main profit from 'hand-to-mouth or salary-cheque-to-salary-cheque middle class. Perhaps a young Civil Servant needs a few pounds for renewing his suburban season ticket. He owns a dress suit that comes out twice a year, for the tennis club dance and the Old Boys' dinner, and he pawns it temporarily to tide him over. Perhaps a young journalist wants a Continental holiday but is on his beam ends; he pawns his typewriter for a month. Perhaps the mother finds the school fees run her short of ready cash; she pawns a fur stole for the summer months and hopes to redeem it for the winter.'

And for this type of trade far fewer pawnshops were required. If someone was pledging an article on which they were getting a loan of fifty pounds, a hundred pounds or more, it was worth going five miles in order to carry out the transaction, whereas a journey of this length made no sense if all one had to pawn was a bundle of washing or a flat-iron for half a crown. Pawnbroking, in plain terms, was going up in the world. It was becoming more of a middle-class affair. Those who realised this and who had taken steps to cater for the new kind of customer were doing well. The others were going to the wall. One might even go so far as to say that the Welfare State was creating a new breed of hard-up people, for whom, as *The Times* put it, 'the three brass balls now and then shine warm as suns in a long winter of recurring bills'.

But for one or two pawnbrokers in London, Edinburgh and other major cities, middle and upper-class customers were nothing new. They had had plenty of them before the Second World War. This was certainly the situation in Edinburgh as early as the 1890s. In 1898 James Duns Quin, who had premises in 6 Crosscauseway, gave evidence before the Lord Provost in a case involving the proposed use of another property in the city for pawnbroking purposes. He said that about a third of his 50,000 separate pledges a year were for jewellery and silver and pointed out that 'There are now several pawnbrokers in Edinburgh who are able to undertake large transactions.' He went on to say: 'There is now not only competition between pawnbrokers in Edinburgh, but competition between pawnbrokers in Edinburgh and other towns. People come from other towns to pawn in Edinburgh and people in Edinburgh go to other towns to pawn. I have had experience myself of persons sending goods to me from London to be pawned, and I have had jewellery sent to me by post from Nice. The pawnbroking business in recent years has changed considerably in its character and in its methods.'[6]

Mr S. E. Wort worked for Horace Bull, Walter Bull's son, at his Theobalds Road shop, from 1925 until 1940, when the premises were destroyed in an air raid. Horace Bull was comfortably off and well educated. During the 1914–18 war he served in France as an officer in the Honourable Artillery Company. He lived near Guildford, where he was able to indulge his taste for gardening, and enjoy his collections of porcelain and paintings. He came up to London two or three times a week. In the very select pawnbroking establishment in Theobalds Road, Mr Wort remembers[7] there regularly came through its doors 'titled people, generals, a Marquis – to pawn his guns and fishing rods, always redeemed at the proper season – doctors and medical students, actors, boxers – to pawn their Lonsdale Belts – bookmakers. Customers of long standing would always stay for a while and chat. The ladies of the town, from Soho and Bloomsbury, were good customers. They used to pawn something and then spend part of the money buying something else from us, usually jewellery.'

It is interesting that Mr Bull should have been an officer. In the First World War few pawnbrokers or pawnbrokers' assistants reached commissioned rank and the same was true in the Second World War. Year by year, between 1940 and 1945, *The Pawnbrokers' Gazette* published the names of members of the trade who were serving with the forces. The list for 1942 was typical. Out of approximately 500 men, there were ten officers, three of whom, somewhat surprisingly, were doctors. The ranks were as follows:

1 Surgeon Captain
1 Surgeon Lieutenant-Commander
1 Surgeon Lieutenant
1 Major
1 Sub-Lieutenant
5 2nd Lieutenants

How many of these officers returned to their pawnbroking activities after the war it is impossible to say. One would particularly like to know about the subsequent careers of the 2nd lieutenants and the sub-lieutenant, who were presumably younger men.

Mr Quin and Mr Bull, however, formed part of a small minority of pawnbrokers, those with the reputation and the capital to conduct such business and to maintain contact with the appropriate type of customer. Over the trade as a whole, the change came much later, more gradually and on a less grand scale. The experience of Mr J. S. Millar, of Glasgow, is more typical. Since about 1970, he has noticed among his customers what he describes as 'an increase in salaried persons, small business people and owner-occupiers, with a tiny fraction of professional people – doctors, lawyers, teachers'.[8] Mr Millar believes that the proportion of this type of customer would be greater if the average pawnbroker's premises, 'both inside and out', were more attractive.

The kind of shop Mr Millar evidently has in mind as in urgent need of improvement is the one described by Jim McNally, from Lisburn in Northern Ireland. He went there in 1961 as a clerk, when he was fifteen, and stayed until it closed down in 1969.

> My first impressions [he recalled][9] were slightly daunting as if I had walked into the early twentieth century. The place had a dampish smell, and the shop was generally dark, although there was an area at the end of the extremely long counter which was better lit (although still dim), where my employer would take the more well-off customers, to either bargain over their pledges, or to sell them some of the more expensive items of jewellery. The lighting consisted of three 2' fluorescent fittings over a 20' counter. My employer was an elderly man – I would say in his 70s – who hobbled about with an old black walking stick, and always complained about his leg or his lumbago. The ailments, however, seemed to rapidly disappear when the occasion called for it, such as chasing off youngsters who would come in looking for loans on their gym-slippers, etc, while they played truant, or whenever the more élite type of customer would come into the shop he would suddenly straighten.

Mr McNally enjoyed the friendly atmosphere of the place:

> We had a kind of relationship with our regular customers which seemed to be almost like that of a priest or a private counsellor. Even with all the so-called benefits available today, I feel the local pawnshop was a very essential part of life in those days, and unwittingly assisted people in learning the value of money, and encouraged wise spending and allocation of available

funds. They helped to knit the local community in a common bond, in much the same way that the local pub does.

This, alas, was a story without a happy ending. The son became impatient with his father's old-fashioned ideas, and pawning became more and more a side-line. Mr McNally saw it all happen.

As the years went on the pawnshop did become more of a general business, selling new equipment such as jewellery, photographic equipment, and ladies' and gents' shoes. This was mainly due to my boss's son having more and more to do with the business and he wanted to gradually eliminate the pawn-broking end of things. He was a primary school master with a lot of ideas for the future, and he introduced new lighting in the shop, glass counters – which were detested by our locals – and went into selling office chairs and desks to the school authorities, using the contacts he had built up as a school teacher.

And eventually, with the old man gone, the business closed. The moral here is not that modernisation is a bad thing, but that this particular community was unsuited to the kind of business the son with ideas wanted to do.

It would be wrong, however, to suppose that poverty and hardship ended abruptly with the outbreak of war and the disappearance of unemployment. The old world did not suddenly vanish at the wave of a magician's wand, and prices and values remained substantially at their pre-war level until the Sixties. In 1950, a shilling was still real money, and one could buy something worth having with it.

For those who believe that the Welfare State started in 1939, the family history of Mrs Kathleen Earp of Bradford should come as a considerable surprise. Mrs Earp's mother was left a widow in 1941, with two young children to support entirely on her own. She had a pension of 7s. 6d. a week and she reckoned to raise another 3s. a week by pawning the few items she had available. 'We were,' says Mrs Earp, 'constantly in debt, until my elder sister left school in 1957. By that time, Mum was also able to find work herself, so we had two wages coming in.'[10]

The pawnbroker's manager was

> . . . a hard, but kind man. He was good to Mum, because he knew what a difficult time she was having with Dad dying at such a

127

young age. She had no chance of getting on her feet. Sometimes he wouldn't lend on items such as sheets, but we had nothing of value to offer. I can see now that there was no value to him in second-hand sheets.

Pride made people ashamed of going to the pawnbroker, even when so many people were in the same boat. Some of our neighbours didn't mind Mum knowing, because she had too much on her mind to want to judge anyone. They knew she couldn't have any pride about it herself. She had no choice.

Those very moving words were written, it is as well to remind ourselves, of the 1940s, not fifty years earlier, and they refer to a woman who was only in her twenties at the time. It was, one might say, the old pawnbroking world having almost its last fling, the world of the pawnshop round the corner and close personal relationships, the world of Uncle.

Some pawnbrokers saw the new world coming surprisingly early, The official list of Pawnbrokers' Certificates for Sheffield for 1925 and 1926 shows that William Hugh Parker, of 17 Middlewood Road, did not renew his licence in 1926. Commenting on this, his son, W. J. Parker, says:

> The pawnbroking was given up in 1925, when my father was twenty-one, he and his brother having a dislike for the sad human side, together with a feeling that the credit schemes beginning to appear in the shops might eventually have an effect on pawnbroking. They went over entirely to retailing, and in 1935 Men's and Boys' wear was separated from jewellery, which moved into No. 19 next door.[11]

Here is another insight into what was happening to pawnbroking in the post-war period. In 1945 Mrs Chamberlain and her husband bought what seemed to be a flourishing business. This, in her own words, is what developed afterwards.[12]

> In 1945 it was a very busy shop, long established. Queues formed on a Monday morning two or three deep in all weathers, waiting for opening time. Most customers were working-class regulars, with suits, shoes, in fact any article to be pledged for a few shillings. On Saturdays most clothes would be redeemed for the weekend.
>
> After a few years, redevelopment started and people were

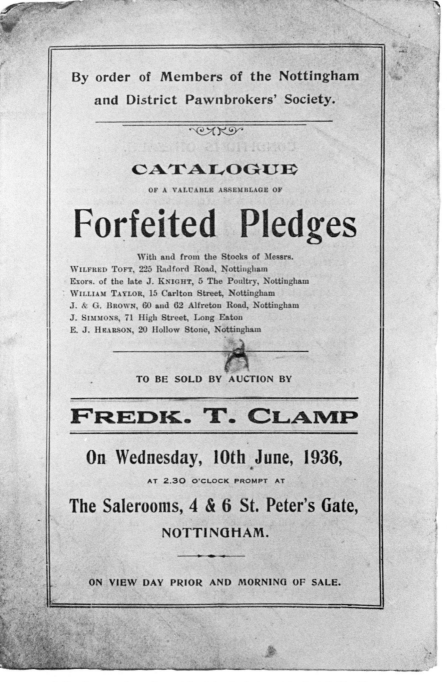

By order of Members of the Nottingham
and District Pawnbrokers' Society.

CATALOGUE

OF A VALUABLE ASSEMBLAGE OF

Forfeited Pledges

With and from the Stocks of Messrs.

WILFRED TOFT, 225 Radford Road, Nottingham

Exors. of the late J. KNIGHT, 5 The Poultry, Nottingham

WILLIAM TAYLOR, 15 Carlton Street, Nottingham

J. & G. BROWN, 60 and 62 Alfreton Road, Nottingham

J. SIMMONS, 71 High Street, Long Eaton

E. J. HEARSON, 20 Hollow Stone, Nottingham

TO BE SOLD BY AUCTION BY

FREDK. T. CLAMP

On Wednesday, 10th June, 1936,

AT 2.30 O'CLOCK PROMPT AT

The Salerooms, 4 & 6 St. Peter's Gate,

NOTTINGHAM.

ON VIEW DAY PRIOR AND MORNING OF SALE.

16 Catalogue of auction of forfeited pledges, Frederick T. Clamp,
Nottingham, 1936 (cover).

BANKERS, NATIONAL BANK LTD., BELGRAVIA, S.W.I.
BUSINESS HOURS: MON TO FRI 9-5

ORIGINAL BUSINESS
ESTABLISHED 1800

Contract

156, Victoria Street (Opposite Underground Station, Victoria,

TELEGRAPHIC ADDRESS 'Polemos' London SW1
TELEPHONE NUMBER 01-834 0310 & 9567

T. M. SUTTON, LIMITED,

I   have deposited with T. M. Sutton
Limited (hereinafter called 'the Pledgee' which shall include its assigns)   the
undermentioned articles which I declare are my own property absolutely

(hereinafter called 'the Pledge') to be held by the Pledgee as a security for the
repayment of £   lent on the   day of
            19   by the Pledgee to me together with interest thereon
from such day at the rate of   per centum per annum which sum I
agree to repay together with interest thereon at the rate aforesaid until
payment. If the right or title of myself or of the Pledgee to the pledge be put into
question or disputed by any person whomsoever or be the subject of or affected by any
legal proceedings whatsoever I authorize the Pledgee to incur such costs and expenses
as it may reasonably think fit in defending or protecting such right or title thereto
and the full amount of such costs and expenses so incurred is to be also a further charge
on the pledge and recoverable from me by the Pledgee as a debt and if the said sum of
£   with interest as aforesaid be not repaid by the   day of
            next I further authorize the Pledgee to dispose of the pledge by sale either
by public auction or private contract and out of the proceeds to pay all expenses of and
incidental to such sale and retain the said amount of £   and
interest as aforesaid and the amount of all costs and expenses incurred in or about
defending or protecting the pledge as aforesaid and all amounts to which the Pledgee
may be entitled under (5) below. The Pledgee to be at liberty (1) to postpone the sale of
the pledge until such time or times as it may think fit (2) to bid for and purchase
the pledge or any portion thereof at such sale by auction and upon such purchase the
Pledgee shall become the absolute owner thereof (3) to deliver up the pledge to any person
delivering to the Pledgee the note or copy now given to me of this Contract (4) To refuse
to deliver up the pledge to me if I do not deliver to the Pledgee such note or copy or
account to the Pledgee's reasonable satisfaction for its non-delivery (5) to charge (a)
the sum of 1/- for the preparation of documents relating to this loan (b) the amount
of any stamp duty paid to the Pledgee upon any of the said documents (c) the sum of 1/-
for rendering (if required) an account of the Sale of the pledge (d) the sum of 1/- in
respect of any inspection of the Pledgee's Books.

No.

Dated this   day of   19

(Signed)

(Address)

17 Contract issued by T. M. Sutton Ltd, 156 Victoria Street,
London, SW1.

Left with William Taylor, 15 Carlton Street, Nottingham

SPECIAL CONTRACTS

SOLD					BOUGHT IN.	
6 10	59	Single-stone diamond ring	... Mar. 34	4	3 10	
	60	9ct. double curb albert	... Nov.	1		
	61	Single-stone diamond ring	...	22	7 10	
9 5	62	Diamond half-hoop ring	...	28		
3 2	63	2-row diamond ring	...	143		
	64	18ct. keyless (case 1 oz. 10½ dwts. gross)	... Dec.	135	7 5	
	65	Diamond Eternity and cluster rings	...	137	5	
	66	14ct. diamond set wristlet (chrome bracelet)	...	171	2 10	
3 12 6	67	3-stone diamond ring	... Jan. 35	22		
	68	9ct. keyless lever, snake ring, wristlet (damaged), opera glasses	...	88	7	
	69	9ct. keyless 17 jewels Record Dreadnought	...	128	3	
8 5	70	Zeiss prism glasses, 6 × 30	...	2355		
	71	18ct. Waltham hunter (1 oz. 1 dwt. case) and dress albert	... Feb.	32	6 15	
	72	Silver coffee pot	...	56	3	
	73	Single-stone diamond ring	...	85	4	
	74	Goerz prism glasses	... Mar.	182	5 10	
	75	Diamond cluster ring	...	191	3	
7 5	76	3-stone diamond ring	... June	113		
3 14	77	9ct. guard and single-stone diamond ring	... Sept. 33	78		
	78	Diamond cluster ring	... Sept. 34	165	2	
2 14	79	Diamond cluster ring	...	2276		
3 16	80	9ct. guard	... Oct.	25		
2 12	81	Prism field glasses in case, 8 × 32	...	53		
	82	9ct. keyless (damaged) and double curb albert	...	85	3 10	
	83	3-stone diamond ring	...	186	1 10	

£50 15 6   £65

Left with J. & G. Brown, 60/62 Alfreton Road, Nottingham.

	84	18ct. single-stone diamond ring	... Mar. 35	159
	85	9ct. gold watch, 15 jewels, on Milanese bracelet	...	170
	86	9ct. wristlet watch, 12320, 15 jewels		171
	87	15ct. dress ring	... Apl.	235
	88	9ct. wristlet watch and two 18ct. dress rings	...	237
	89	18ct. wristlet watch, 1395269, on 15ct. bracelet	...	259
	90	Gent.'s 9ct. gold wrist watch, 272601	...	287
	91	9ct. wristlet watch, 20183	...	299

18 Clamp's auction catalogue, 1936: sample page, showing prices realised.

452

PAWNBROKERS ACT, 1872.
(35 & 36 *Vict. c.* 93.)

PAWNBROKER'S CERTIFICATE.

The COUNCIL OF THE CITY ~~AND COUNTY~~ OF BRISTOL in pursuance

of The Local Government Act, 1894, **do hereby certify** that they authorise the

grant to *A. D ↑ J. D. COOK LTD.*

of *38/40 THE HORSEFAIR* in the said City

~~and County~~ of a Licence to carry on the business of a Pawnbroker within the

City ~~and County~~ of Bristol.

This Licence will expire on the 1st day of July, One thousand nine hundred

and *SEVENTY SEVEN.*

As witness our hand this *8th* day of *July* 19 *76.*

G. R. Robertson

John B. Atonson } *Members of the Council of the City and County of Bristol.*

19 Licence issued to A. D. and J. D. Cook of Bristol, 1976.

rehoused on council estates. We lost most of our trade. Later, the better-class people arrived, to pledge mainly jewellery. They used to travel from out-of-town districts and they used the front shop instead of the back entrance, which had always been the way into the pledging department. They also stopped coming, due no doubt to State Help. Eventually, in 1957, we were forced to close.

Mr Ernest Hush, of Middlesbrough, had a different kind of experience with 'the better-class people'. In 1960, when the 1872 Pawnbrokers' Act was updated and the top limit of any one pledge was raised from ten pounds to fifty pounds, 'the change in our shop was unbelievable. Overnight we acquired a completely new type of customer who had hitherto borrowed from moneylenders at 48% and were only too happy to come to us for 25%.'[13] Mr Hush was able to see this phenomenon for himself, because he had been skilful enough or lucky enough to be a survivor. He had remained in business, with his colleagues closing down all around him, although at a slightly slower rate than during the 1940s, when on the average a hundred pawnbrokers a year had ceased to trade.

The changes brought in by the 1960 Act were the result of very hard work on the part of the Association. At the Annual Conference in 1955, the Council was given a mandate to proceed with a scheme to revise the Act. Four members of the Council were appointed to carry out the task. There were visits to government departments to prove the Association's case for revising the 1872 Act, balance sheets were obtained from pawnbrokers all over the country, interviews were arranged with MPs and eventually a draft Bill was prepared. Its passage through Parliament was unusually speedy: it became law in thirteen weeks.

The Act permitted considerable changes in the grading of pledges and in the length of time allowed before forfeiture. There were three grades – A, under 40s.; B, 40s. to £5; C, from £5 to £50 – and all were for six months only, instead of twelve, as previously.

The passage of the Bill through the Lords produced some particularly interesting speeches and exchanges of view. The ground had been well prepared and pawnbrokers must have been both pleased and surprised to find that they had so many influential friends who were willing to support them in public. Chief among them were Mr (later Sir) R. Graham Page, who steered the Bill through the Commons and Lord Meston who presented it to the Upper House.

> Unless we do something to help 'dear old Uncle' [he said], he will rapidly go out of business altogether. How would your Lordships like to be remunerated on the same basis as you were remunerated in 1872? Let me give your Lordships an example of what is happening in the business of pawnbroking. Take the case of a pawnbroker using a capital of £5,000. The average gross receipts are probably about twenty-five per cent in a year – that is to say, gross receipts of £1,250 per annum. He will have to employ a manager, an assistant and a junior assistant. In addition to the wages of those persons, the pawnbroker has to pay out of his £1,250 the rent, rates, insurance, lighting, heating, printing and all the rest of the shop and overhead expenses. If your Lordships think that that leaves him with any profit, then you are more optimistic than I am.[14]

The passage of the Irish Pawnbrokers Bill through the Dail and Senate in 1964 was much more acrimonious. Irish pawnbrokers were still controlled by the Statutes of 1786 and 1788, which bore little relation to current problems and conditions, and there was obviously a strong case for bringing the law up-to-date.

The 1872 Act, which did not apply to Ireland, had left English pawnbrokers in a much more favourable situation. The Irish pawn-brokers had three major grievances. In 1872 all restrictions on the opening hours of pawnbroking establishments had been abolished in England, but not in Ireland. By the same Act, the tax levied on pawnbrokers in London had been reduced from £15 to £7 10s., the existing rate in the provinces. In Ireland it had always been £7 10s., except in Dublin, where it remained at the high and absurd figure of £99 18s. 1¾d. The third complaint was that after 1872 the pawn ticket in England contained, by law, all the necessary in-formation concerning the scale of charges and terms of redemption. This was not so in Ireland and a great many misunderstandings and arguments arose from the omission.[15]

The Bill was presented in both the Dail and the Senate by the Minister of Justice, Charles Haughey, who was and is a man accustomed to getting his own way and to dealing somewhat roughly and abruptly with the opposition.

In the Dail, Mr Haughey defended pawnbroking in these terms:

It may be held by some that pawnbroking is dying out and that nothing should be done to keep it alive. I do not accept this view. Pawnbrokers have provided a very useful service to the community in the past. It is true that the statistics available reveal a steady decline over recent years in the demand for the services offered by pawnbrokers – a decline which reflects the general improvement in the level of wages and employment and the expansion of credit facilities in other directions. Despite these improvements, however, I believe there will still be room for the special loan facilities provided by pawnbrokers. These facilities can be made all the more efficient and the interests of pawners better protected if the law governing pawnbroking is simplified and brought up to date, as the Bill proposes to do.[16]

Dr Browne, however, saw the Bill as an irrelevance. He wanted pawnbroking to wither away and die.

I think it is wrong that so many families do find it necessary to use the pawnbroker's establishment. It is essentially a sordid substitute for social justice and our people should not be placed in this position. I think the Minister, in bringing in this type of legislation, is tacitly accepting the continued existence of this kind of establishment in our society for some considerable time to come. If he were satisfied that there was to be a continued expansion in our economy, our affluence, then he would not find it necessary to confront the House at this time with this amendment to antiquated legislation.[17]

Mr Haughey, however, pushed the Bill through the Dail in his usual brisk style, but he had more trouble with the Senate. Mr Murphy said that he would like to see 'this disgraceful business disappear altogether' and urged the Minister 'to devote his energies to seeing that the three balls will no longer dominate some of our streets and provide this public exhibition on Monday mornings'.[18]

The Senate refused to accept Mr Haughey's recommendation, considered it had been treated peremptorily and with discourtesy, and divided on the issue, after Professor Hayes had said, 'This division has been caused by the Minister's very insolent action. I am voting against his insolent attitude. He has been convenienced, no end, here tonight and he has treated us with insolence, without a vestige of good manners. This, therefore, is a vote against the Minister for his attitude. It is disgraceful.'[19] The Senate rejected the Bill, with Professor Hayes saying, 'Good manners pay good dividends,' and Mr Haughey muttering, 'It will pass just the same,' which it eventually did.

The proceedings of the Irish Parliament make much better reading than their British equivalent. Speakers tend to be more direct and have a finer flow of language. When the Dail and the Senate debated pawnbroking, real feelings come to the surface and we begin to understand something of the trade's public image in Ireland. The House of Commons and the House of Lords did not provide quite the same service for Britain in 1960.

But the continued decline of pawnbroking has been common to both countries during the second half of the century. The substantial and continuing reduction in the number of pawnbrokers since the Thirties had important practical consequences for the Association. The demise of *The Pawnbrokers' Gazette* was a sad result of the Association's falling membership. The last issue, No. 6303, was published at the end of December 1958. It had been appearing weekly since October 1838 and had the distinction of being the oldest trade paper in the country. Unfortunately, because it is such a wonderfully rich quarry of information for the social historian, it is also one of the most difficult periodicals to consult. Only two files of any consequence are known to exist, and neither is complete. The series held by the National Pawnbrokers' Association itself lacks the first forty years' issues, a tantalising gap, and the one in the British Library at Colindale is even more deficient. If this note should result in copies, particularly of the earlier issues, being discovered elsewhere, historians would have real reasons to be grateful.

The *Gazette* was succeeded by a less ambitious venture, the *NPA Journal*, which appeared first monthly, then every two months and then, as at present, quarterly, and which is still in existence. It was the *Journal*, not the *Gazette*, which had the sad duty of reporting the sale, in 1973, of that great monument to the old days of pawning by the masses, Lombard House. The site was wanted by the City of London for a redevelopment scheme, but there have been long delays over this and the now rather forlorn building is, in fact, still standing. It was sold privately for £210,000 – a compulsory purchase order by the City of London would have yielded less – and the offices of the Association, of the Pawnbrokers' Charitable Institution, and of the Metropolitan Pawnbrokers' Protection Society were transferred to Southend-on-Sea.

Lombard House was always, in fact, too big for the Association's needs. As a dream, it rather overreached itself. It consisted of a basement, ground floor and four floors above. Apart from the strong-room in the basement, the ground floor front office and the Council Chamber on the first floor, all the remaining office space was let to tenants, many of whom established a long connection with the building.

When the building was originally opened in the mid-Twenties, the front office was intended to be a reception lounge, where members could meet and hold interviews, but this idea never materialised to any extent and the room soon became the General Secretary's office.

After Lombard House had been sold, the Association published the following statement for the benefit of its members.

> The rental income, after allowing for the costs of lighting, heating, general repairs and lift maintenance, helped to defray the working expenses of the Association but in recent years the rising maintenance expenses were having a serious effect on income. Indeed, had the Association remained in occupation for many more years it would have been faced with modernisation costs amounting to many thousands of pounds. In fact, expert opinion recommended a complete interior rebuilding scheme and subsequent leasing of the entire building to one tenant.[20]

The Board Room furniture and certain other items from Lombard House were transferred to the headquarters of Harvey & Thompson Ltd., in South London, where they are in daily use and well looked after. More will be said about Harvey & Thompson in the next chapter, but it is interesting to observe here that, amid the general story of dignified decline which has inevitably characterised the *Journal* for some years, there is always the quite different tone of the news from Harvey & Thompson, which has been about expansion and success, not contraction and trading-on-the-defensive. In 1974, for example, we have the announcement of a new branch in High Street, Orpington,[21] and in 1977, the Company's Annual Report, printed here as usual, contains the cheerful news that 'the sharp upsurge in pawnbroking has continued.'[22]

But, however good a firm's management may be and however progressive and imaginative its ideas, pawnbroking can only survive and prosper if it can attract and hold suitable staff. In July 1969, W. H. Moore Ltd., a large and old-established Newcastle firm, closed its last three shops. 'Moore's say they are closing because it is impossible to find and train staff. Nobody is learning the trade any more, and the decision to close came, paradoxically, at a time when the firm was busier than ever before.'[23] 'There is difficulty in recruiting staff,' reported A. L. Minkes, of the London School of Economics in 1953, 'because of distaste for the trade, and an acute shortage of experienced men.'[24]

An advertisement, inserted in the *NPA Journal* in 1973, tells its own story. It came from a London pawnbroker, A. C. Lucombe Ltd.

> Man, any age, with or without experience . . . as assistant to jeweller and pawnbroker (no clothing). Must be trustworthy, good references essential. 5 day week. 3 weeks' holiday. Rent-free unfurnished flat with free gas and electricity available if required.[25]

The flight from the trade began immediately after the Second World War. C. R. Pocklington, of Mexborough, was one of the people who left, and he is quite clear why. 'After the war,' he wrote, 'people seemed to view pawnbroking as a really sordid business and didn't want any part of it. Staff of any kind was difficult to obtain, and anyone who was employed by David Haigh[26] before the war and had returned, soon left, including me.'[27]

Pawnbrokers themselves might speak and write of the valuable service which they provided to the community and of their reasonable charges but, in a free labour market, the plain fact was that the trade was simply unable to attract the right type of recruit. The pre-war stigma, however unfair and unjustified it may have been, was still very much a reality among young people and their parents. To most people it was, in Mr Pocklington's words, the 'sordid business'. The Association's President, Mr C. Suttenstall, was absolutely right when he said, at the Conference in Bath in 1978, 'We need new blood of the right type – profitable trade to enable us to pay a good living wage to good efficient youngsters. Pawnbroking *must* stand out as a most interesting vocation among the service trades.'[28] It is, of course, a circular argument. Pawnbroking must be profitable in order to be able to get the kind of staff it needs, and it must have the right kind of staff in order to be profitable, or indeed to exist at all. The ways in which a few modern-minded firms have managed to break the circle will be discussed in the next chapter. It is in their achievement that the main hope for the future lies. Staff who come and go are useless. To acquire the necessary technical and legal knowledge, to say nothing of the experience of people and their habits, takes a long time, and without it a person is not of much use to his employer, nor is he worth a good salary. Since 1945 the labour situation has been a more critical, though less discussed and publicised problem than interest rates and profitability. And, as the following pages argue, the ability to recruit and hold good staff is closely bound up with modernisation and the creation of an up-to-date image of the trade.

NOTES

1 These statistics have been provided by the Association, with a warning that they do not correspond exactly to the actual number of Customs and Excise licences in force, since not all pawnbrokers have been members of their local society. One can safely assume, however, that up to 1940, at least ninety per cent would have been members, and since 1960, ninety-five per cent.
2 The figure for this year only covers the whole of Scotland.
3 The figure for this year only covers the whole of Northern Ireland.
4 22 June 1957.
5 17 February 1950.
6 *Proceedings in reference to the Equitable Loan Company of Scotland*, before the Lord Provost, Magistrates and Council of the City of Edinburgh. Seventh Day, Friday, 14 October 1898.
7 Information sent to the author, 11 November 1980.
8 Information sent to the author, 10 March 1981.
9 Information sent to the author, 2 December 1980.
10 Information supplied to the author, 8 January 1981.
11 Information sent to the author, 3 April 1981.
12 Information sent to the author, 5 January 1981.
13 Information sent to the author, 1 January 1981.
14 *Hansard*, 22 March 1960, column 72.
15 On this, see W. Neilson Hancock, 'On the extension of the laws of pawnbroking now in force in Great Britain to Ireland', *Journal of the Statistical and Social Inquiry Society of Ireland*, December 1876.
16 Dail Eireann: *Proceedings*, 18 February 1964, column 1118.
17 Dail Eireann: *Proceedings*, 18 February 1964, column 1133.
18 Seanad Eireann: *Proceedings*, 1 July 1964, column 1408.
19 Seanad Eireann: *Proceedings*, 1 July 1964, column 1408.
20 *NPA Journal*, August 1973.
21 *NPA Journal*, October 1974.
22 *NPA Journal*, October 1977.
23 *Newcastle Evening Chronicle*, 9 June 1969.
24 A. L. Minkes, 'The Decline of Pawnbroking', *Economica*, February 1953.
25 *NPA Journal*, February 1973.
26 A large Yorkshire business with fourteen shops.
27 Information supplied to the author, 13 January 1981.
28 *NPA Journal*, June 1978.

8

A Future for Pawnbroking?

There have always been great dangers in making generalised statements about pawnbroking. Conditions have varied a great deal between one district and one business and another and 'the average pawnbroker' is probably as mythical a figure as 'the average farmer'. The variables – the age of the proprietor, the availability or non-availability of family labour, the skill with which the retail side of the shop or shops has been run, ability to recruit skilled staff, the changing character of the district – have conditioned the relative success of the business. Even so, a broad distinction between two types of pawnbroking has persisted for perhaps two hundred years, the division between what is known in the trade as city and industrial pawning, the first being concerned with jewellery, watches and plate, and the second with clothing, bedding and domestic articles of all kinds.

As late as the 1950s, most pawnbroking establishments, perhaps as high a proportion as seventy-five per cent, could be broadly classed as industrial, in the sense that most of their pledges were of the domestic variety. The average loan was under a pound. Among pawnbrokers doing a mixed business, the usual non-industrial loan was not more than ten pounds, the figure above which a pawnbroker required a moneylender's licence.

The profit on the pawnbroking side of a business has not been high, at least since the First World War. One authority has estimated that the gross profit rate on turnover – the total amount of money lent during the year – rarely exceeded seven per cent, with the net profit not likely to be more than half this.[1] In the industrial trade, the basis of success was a very large number of pledges frequently turned over. During a period of economic depression, such as the 1930s, certain other factors had to be taken into account. More people wanted to pawn their goods, but fewer were able to redeem them, so that the pawnbroker would find himself with a difficult financial problem, with stocks accumulating of goods he was unable to attempt to sell until the statutory period of twelve months and seven days had elapsed. Eventually, however, he would have available for sale goods which he had acquired at very low prices and which he could afford to market at prices which undercut those charged in other shops. The more severe the recession, the less he could advance on each article, since his own capital was not elastic.

Between the wars it was not exceptional for industrial pawnbrokers to take in 2,000 pledges a week and some managed to deal with even more. By the 1950s, however, virtually no pawnbroker was doing this volume of business. Minkes,[2] writing in 1953, reckoned that in industrial pawnbroking at that time the usual number of pledges ranged from 300 to 600 a week, with the total sum loaned annually usually being of the order of £10,000 to £15,000 and, in a few cases, as much as £20,000. In the mixed trade, with jewellery and other high-value goods amounting to half the total amount loaned – possibly a generous figure – the pawnbroking turnover was occasionally in excess of £50,000 and, for certain businesses engaged in the city trade, to considerably more than this. These figures refer to individual shops, not to firms. Assuming Minkes's estimates to be reliable – they were based on as careful research as was possible – a pawnbroker's gross profits in the early Fifties can be reckoned to have been £700 at the bottom end and £3,500 at the top, with net profit running at, say, £350 to £1,750. It is obvious that, without a substantial retailing side to supplement his income, very few pawnbrokers could have afforded to continue and many did in fact decide to close for precisely this reason. The expenses of the trade were high. Rent and rates had to be paid and at least adequate staff employed. Clerical costs for a large volume of small, short-period loans were considerable, and the bulkier pledges were expensive to store. It is worth mentioning that pawnbrokers have always preferred to avoid bank loans or other outside sources as a means of financing their business. They have traditionally relied on their own capital resources to cover their loans to customers.

From the evidence he was able to obtain, Minkes came to the

conclusion that, at the date of his research, about 400,000 people a year were making use of a pawnbroker's services. Assuming that the average family consisted of four persons, this meant that the number of people whose lives were directly or indirectly touched by pawnbroking amounted to about three per cent of the population of Great Britain or, putting the matter the other way round, that ninety-seven per cent had no recent or regular acquaintance with pawnbroking.

In the late Sixties, believing that the trade would virtually disappear if something was not done to make it possible for pawnbrokers to earn bigger profits, the National Pawnbrokers' Association prepared a draft Bill to increase the statutorily permitted rate of interest. This was overtaken by history, since by that time the Government had decided to overhaul and simplify the whole of the complex system of legislation which regulated the provision of credit. A great deal of preliminary investigation was carried out before the new Consumer Credit Bill was drafted. This included commissioning NOP Market Research Ltd. to carry out a survey of the trade, based on a twenty per cent sample.[3] Using the results of the survey as its main source of information, the Consumer Credit Committee produced an objective analysis of the situation. Its findings were summed up in the following paragraph:

Most pawnbrokers now in business have been established for twenty years or more and new entrants are few. Some sixty per cent of pawnbrokers are incorporated and the remainder are individual traders (this corresponds to the normal pattern in retail trade generally). Some licensed pawnbrokers are also licensed moneylenders but the number is only about twenty per cent of the total of pawnbrokers and is smaller than might have been expected. On the other hand, something like ninety per cent of pawnbrokers also engage in some type of retailing, most often the sale of jewellery, although other retailing, e.g. of cameras, is frequently found. Auction pledges appear to account for most business, with low pledges under ten per cent of the total and special contracts under twenty per cent. The average low pledge is about 20s. to 25s., the average auction pledge between three pounds to four pounds and the average special contract between ten pounds and fifteen pounds. Under ten per cent of pledges appear to be repledged at once on redemption.

The goods most often pledged still include clothing but jewellery is far and away the most important and sports equipment, radios, tape recorders, cameras, musical instruments and furs are all now important. Immediately after Christmas tends to be the busiest season, but trade is fairly evenly spread throughout the year. Perhaps about half of the loans made are to meet difficulties – as a common answer in the survey put it, 'to pay bills' – but the other fifty per cent of loans are said to be more for covering abnormal outlays, as on holidays or weddings or to buy other durable goods.[4]

The Consumer Credit Act was finally approved by Parliament on 31 July 1974. It is described in the preamble as 'An Act to establish for the protection of consumers a new system, administered by the Director General of Fair Trading, of licensing, and other control of traders concerned with the provision of credit, or the supply of goods on hire or hire-purchase, and their transactions, in place of the present enactments regulating moneylenders, pawnbrokers and hire-purchase traders and their transactions; and for related matters.' It repeals the Pawnbrokers' Acts of 1872 and 1960, the Moneylenders' Acts of 1900 and 1927, the Charitable Pawn Offices (Ireland) Act 1842, the Moneylenders' Act (Northern Ireland) 1933, and the Pawnbrokers' Act (Northern Ireland) 1954. The Act as a whole became law as soon as it was passed, but certain sections, including those referring to pledging, were to come into operation on a day to be appointed. It is expected that, so far as pawnbroking is concerned, this will be some time early in 1983, subject to discussions between the Association and the Director of Fair Trading over certain practical details, especially the kind of documentation which a pawnbroker will require in order to carry out his business in the future.

The new Act lays down that, for all types of credit:

20. (1) The Secretary of State shall make regulations containing such provisions as appear to him appropriate for determining the true cost to the debtor of the credit provided or to be provided under an actual or prospective consumer credit agreement (the 'total charge for credit'), and regulations so made shall prescribe:
(a) what items are to be treated as entering into the total charge for credit, and how their amount is to be ascertained;

(b) the method of calculating the rate of the total charge for credit.

A pawnbroker will, in other words, still operate under a system of controlled charges. He will also be required to obtain a standard form of licence, not peculiar to pawnbrokers, and to demonstrate, for this purpose, that 'he is a fit person to engage in activities covered by the licence'.

It was further ordered that, for anyone involved in the business of consumer credit:

26. Regulations may be made as to the conduct by a licensee of his business, and may in particular specify:

(a) the books and other records to be kept by him, and

(b) the information to be furnished by him to persons with whom he does business or seeks to do business, and the way it is to be furnished.

A pawn is redeemable at any time within six months, unless a longer period has been specifically arranged. 'After the expiry of five days following the end of the redemption period' the pawnbroker must give the pawner notice in writing of his intention to sell the goods, 'indicating in the notice the asking price and such other particulars as may be prescribed'. Once the sale has taken place, the original owner must be notified, again in writing, of the proceeds of the sale and the expenses involved. The pawnbroker is then to pay the person who pledged the article with him whatever amount has resulted from the sale after the amount of the loan and all charges have been deducted.

These are, of course, early days and it is impossible to say at the moment exactly how the Act will work out in practice. What is certain, however, is that the pawnbroker is going to be involved in a great deal more paperwork in the future and that this extra burden is bound to add to his overheads and to change the way in which he organises his business. Correspondence from a pawnbroker, which will henceforth be obligatory once a pledge has not been redeemed, may not always be a welcome addition to the domestic mail, especially perhaps in those cases where a wife has pawned goods without her husband's knowledge.

Every effort has naturally been made to ensure that the documentation is as simple and straightforward as possible, but it seems inevitable that a pawnbroker's office will have to be organised in a different way in order to deal efficiently with the new kind of demands made on it. It can be fairly said that the provisions of the new Act would have been completely unworkable if the old system of high-volume industrial pawning had continued. The sheer number of transactions involved would have put an intolerable pressure on the staff and in any case the clerical costs would have been more than the business could have absorbed, while the average value of a pledge was so small. Pledges, in other words, had to be far less in number and far higher in value before pawnbrokers could be expected to meet the requirements of the 1974 Act.

But, even now, the Act seems likely to accelerate certain trends which have already become observable. One might even be bold enough to indulge in a limited amount of prophecy. The large business, with a number of branches, will usually be much better placed to organise the office work which today's flow of paper demands. No pawnbroking business so far makes use of a computer for the purpose of maintaining records, but this stage of modernisation cannot be long delayed. The place for keeping records and carrying out correspondence nowadays is in a properly equipped headquarters office, not at the point where business is transacted with members of the public. Only on this basis will it be possible to engage and pay the kind of specialist staff required. Procedures will have to be standardised, so that the people employed in the shops, buying and selling goods and valuing and accepting pledges, are free to use their skills in a way that justifies their salary. Businesses which continue to try to operate in a way appropriate to the 1930s are not likely to survive much longer.

It may well be, of course, that, once the practical implications of the Consumer Credit Act are fully realised, many individual pawnbrokers will decide that the pledging trade is simply not worth all the trouble involved and concentrate all their energies and capital on the retailing side of their business. It is equally possible that people with no previous experience of pawnbroking will see considerable attractions in this form of credit, and will move capital and business expertise into catering for it. The Consumer Credit Act refers throughout to pledging, not pawnbroking. This may be a significant pointer to the future. There seems to be no particular reason why the trade should not continue and prosper and the name disappear. This could have real advantages. The old associations of pawnbroking with poverty and misery would be swept out of the way and the emphasis would be on the practical value of being able to obtain immediate cash by leaving one's possessions as security.

There are certainly many people who would regret this, as there are those who look back longingly to the good old days when the banks kept their books on the spot in hand-written ledgers and knew nothing of computers and day-by-day centralised control, and when bank managers were masters in their own house. There are many others who similarly lament the disappearance of the small grocer and butcher and detest the impersonal self-service affairs which have taken their place. But the spirit of the age is conditioned by the need for high productivity from expensive labour and for methods of dealing as efficiently and painlessly as possible with the twin nuisances of paper and bureaucracy. It is highly unlikely that pawnbroking will be able to stand aside from the general trend of business. It provides a service which is still required and for which, given professional skill and imagination, the demand can probably be increased.

There are now sufficient pointers to the future to make reasonably confident suggestions as to what is likely to happen during the next ten or twenty years. We could usefully regard two businesses, one in London and the other in Dublin, as laboratories of pawnbroking. In London, the old-established firm of Harvey & Thompson has been undergoing a quiet but unmistakable transformation in recent years. It has a young and enthusiastic managing director who is convinced that pawnbroking has a real future and who is prepared to commit his own career to developing the kind of pawnbroking which is suited to today's conditions. He sees the problem as essentially one of style. A modern pawnbroker is trying to attract business from people who are familiar with banks, building societies, airports and good shops, all of which pay much attention to the impression created by their premises. If he is to succeed, his approach must avoid giving his customers the slightest feeling that they are slumming or losing face by patronising him. There must be nothing to suggest poverty or a fall in social status.

To get the details right must involve constant experiment, and Harvey & Thompson regard their Golders Green shop in this light. The questions they are asking themselves all the time are crucial to the future of the business – 'Is the colour scheme suit-

143

able?' 'Do customers approve of the furnishings and the magazines in the waiting area?' 'Does the façade impress passers-by in the way it should?' 'Have the staff got the appearance, voice, personality and technique to put middle-class people at ease?' By deliberately seeking to find the answers to these questions and by quickly making any changes which may be required, the firm should be able to open future branches with much greater confidence. Development will take place on a basis of research, not guesswork.

Meanwhile, an hour or so spent at Golders Green as an observer reveals as great a contrast to the old type of pawnbroking business as one could possibly imagine. The atmosphere is extremely quiet and one's first impression is that the staff, one man and one woman, both young and with an extremely easy, pleasant manner, have remarkably little work to do. The occasional customer comes in to bring or redeem a pledge, the business is dealt with quickly and easily, and there are fairly long periods of relaxation, when the staff occupy themselves with reading or conversation. But this branch does, in fact, transact thousands of pounds worth of profitable business each day and completely without fuss or rush, because individual pledges are mostly for substantial sums. There is time to pay proper attention to every customer.

The only storage space is the strong room: the new type of pawnbroking premises do not need to be extensive, because the goods taken in are all of small bulk and high value. The staff have been carefully selected, both for their previous experience and for their potential. The manager is jewellery-trained, and he could easily find himself an excellent position in that line of business if he should happen to tire of pledging one day. Meanwhile, however, he feels his present work is extremely satisfying, and enjoys the human aspects of it very much. He is clearly earmarked for promotion and he is unlikely, one would suppose, to spend more than a few years at Golders Green. For him, it is important that he is working for a large and expanding concern, so that he can move upwards without being compelled to change his employer.

The managing director of Harvey & Thompson, Philip Murphy, is as different in appearance, manner and tastes from the traditional stereotype of a pawnbroker as one could possibly imagine, with the good looks and style of dressing of a young French or Italian film actor. One recalls Sir Arthur Conan Doyle's descrip-

20 Exterior of Harvey & Thompson's new shop in Golders Green,
which has no retail department.

21 Interior of Harvey & Thompson's new shop,
showing pledging counter.

22 Modern interior of W. Taylor's shop in Nottingham, showing type and
quality of goods for sale.

tion of a pawnbroker, Jabez Wilson – '. . . an average commonplace British tradesman, obese, pompous and slow. He wore rather baggy grey shepherd's check trousers, a not over-clean black frock-coat, unbuttoned in the front, and a drab waistcoat with a heavy brassy Albert chain and a square pierced bit of metal dangling down as an ornament'[5] – and one realises that times have indeed changed. In the time of Charles Dickens and Sir Arthur Conan Doyle, the British pawnbroker, at least so far as journalists and writers of fiction were concerned, was primarily the London pawnbroker, and the stereotype such writers created for the benefit of the public, but hardly of the trade itself, was an unflattering combination of the vulgar and the sinister, the provider of funds for the poor, the more than occasional receiver of stolen goods, the occupier of dingy and far from clean premises. The National Pawnbrokers' Association fought for three-quarters of a century to correct this image and to draw attention to the number of pawnbrokers who had played an active and distinguished part in public life, giving their services for the benefit of the community in the same way as members of other trades and professions have done. The Association has been able to point to an impressive series of Lord Mayors, magistrates and Justices of the Peace, and to at least two Members of Parliament, Sir Walter Womersley, MP, a Grimsby pawnbroker, and Sir J. Smedley Crooke, MP, a leading representative of the trade in Birmingham. There has also been more than one pawnbroker who has become well known as a result of his hobby, such as the internationally famous seismologist, J. J. Shaw of West Bromwich.

But, once firmly established, a stereotype is exceedingly difficult to dislodge or replace, however wildly inaccurate or even libellous it may be. As the late Sir Mortimer Wheeler once pointed out, there are always two parallel forms of history, one based on accurate scholarship and the other on myth, legend and sensationalism. The public always tends to prefer the myth. Sir Walter Womersley, MP, pawnbroker of Grimsby, is bound to come a poor second in the popular mind and the popular press to William Sheward, pawnbroker of Norwich, who in 1851 murdered his wife and cut her into pieces on the pledging counter.[6] The creation of a new public image for an individual or an organisation is a highly skilled and, under today's conditions, a very costly business.

But one has to begin image-building somewhere and nowadays

that somewhere is usually on television. So far, pawnbrokers have appeared only very rarely in this way, although rather more often on radio, so that most members of the general public have never seen a pawnbroker at all. The appearance of Mr Murphy or some other up-to-date representative of the trade on the screen is likely to give many viewers a considerable surprise.

In those cases where a pawnbroking office is combined with a jewellery retail shop, it is essential that the two sides of the business should present the same image. The goods that are pledged must bear a reasonably close resemblance to the goods that are sold, the people who pawn must not be too different from the people who buy. Broadly speaking, this has always been the case. In the days when most of what pawnbrokers took in consisted of cheap clothing and domestic equipment of one kind and another, this is what they sold in their front shop. As the quality and value of pledges have risen, so, too, has the level of the retail department. But it is not simply a question of what is sold or pledged: the surroundings and atmosphere of the business are equally important and for this reason many pawnbroking establishments nowadays are in new or completely refurbished premises.

A business which is particularly worth studying from this point of view is that of J. B. Brereton in Dublin. Mr Jack Brereton, who took over many years ago from his father, now has two shops. One, in what might be described as Dublin's Bond Street area, is concerned entirely with jewellery. The other, the original business, occupies a very fine Georgian house, with a shop selling good quality jewellery and porcelain on the ground floor and a pledge office in the basement. The pledge office has recently been completely redesigned and refurnished, so that it now presents an appearance remarkably similar to that of Harvey & Thompson in Golders Green or, for that matter, Porritts in Newcastle, or Bowes in Manchester. Mr Jack Brereton now has his two sons working with him in the business. One is a chartered accountant and the other is a Business Studies graduate from Trinity College, Dublin. They represent the new breed of pawnbroker, well qualified, ambitious, and demanding a style of business which they can be proud to show to their friends and contemporaries. They have a middle-class trade, both on street level and in the basement, and they are actively grading it up all the time. The upstairs rooms, formerly used to store low-value pledges, have been emptied of their old racks and have been re-converted to living accommodation which is in keeping with the beauty of the building.

Here, as in Golders Green, people now travel considerable distances to pawn. They come in their cars and the old backyard has been turned into a car park for their convenience. One fairly regular customer drives in to pledge a Chinese Famille Rose bowl, worth several thousands of pounds. Thirty years ago it would have been a local woman with her husband's best suit or her children's boots.

One must, in fairness, say that the traditional pawnbroking world is still in evidence here and there, especially in Scotland, where modernisation has not proceeded as fast as it has south of the Border. A typical Scottish pawn-office still has its private pledging boxes, so suggestive of Victorian and Edwardian attitudes, the dark staircase up to the office, and its racks of pawned goods, although these are likely nowadays to contain working-class luxuries – bags of golf-clubs, piano accordions, transistor radios and sewing machines – rather than working-class necessities.

In conversations with the more adventurous and confident of today's pawnbrokers, one hears a number of interesting possibilities discussed – pledge offices at airports; pledge offices combined with foreign exchange bureaux; a pledge-it-here, redeem-it-there system, rather like car-hire, so that people on holiday could pawn jewellery in, say, Spain and get it back later in one of the firm's branches in Birmingham, perhaps, or Cardiff. It seems unlikely that the banks are going to sit quietly by and watch profitable lending business slip through their fingers. Within the next few years one or two of them may set up pawnbroking subsidiaries, possibly under another name, or they may buy their way in by taking over control of existing firms. Or, just possibly, they may establish discreet pledging facilities at carefully selected branch banks, although this seems rather less likely.

The key to expansion and success is probably staff, not capital. It could be that during the Eighties and Nineties young, intelligent, adaptable men and women, with good experience of the jewellery trade, will find themselves much in demand and as frantically sought after and bribed away from their present employers as computer people were ten years ago.

British pawnbroking has a history that goes back five hundred years. It could quite possibly be in the process of returning to something like its origins, lending money to people who need it to maintain their social position and their standard of living, not to keep themselves from starvation. Its associations with poverty, squalor and despair may be seen, fifty years from now, to have been simply a temporary phase, an historical accident.

NOTES

1 A. L. Minkes, 'The Decline of Pawnbroking', *Economica*, February 1953, p. 14.
2 Op. cit., pp. 19–20.
3 *Moneylenders and Pawnbrokers*. A report on a survey carried out for the Committee on Consumer Credit (The Crowther Committee) by NOP Market Research Limited, July 1970.

   The Survey used a representative sample of 373 moneylenders and 115 pawnbrokers.
4 *Consumer Credit: Report of the Committee*, Vol. I, 1971, 2.4.13.
5 'The Red Headed League', in *The Adventures of Sherlock Holmes*, 1891.
6 The incident took place in 1851, but Sheward was not tried and executed for the crime until eighteen years later, following a voluntary confession to the police. The story is told, in much detail, in *The Retail Jeweller*, 11 December 1980. The counter is still in use, and the founder of the firm of W. and G. Boston, who subsequently took over the business, slept on it when he was an apprentice.

Appendix 1

*The Pawnbrokers' Act, 1872: A Summary**

The Act was not to extend to Ireland. It applied:

'1   To every loan by a Pawnbroker of forty shillings or under.
'2   To every loan by a Pawnbroker of above forty shillings and not above ten pounds, except as in this Act otherwise provided in relation to cases where a special contract respecting the terms of the loan (as authorised by this Act) is made between the pawner and the Pawnbroker at the time of the pawning.

'Nothing in this Act shall apply to a loan by a Pawnbroker of above ten pounds, or to the pledge on which the loan is made, or to the Pawnbroker or pawner in relation to the loan or pledge; and, notwithstanding anything in this Act, a person shall not be deemed a Pawnbroker by reason only of his paying, advancing, or lending on any terms any sum or sums of above ten pounds.'

A pawnbroker was to keep and use certain prescribed books and documents and enter the necessary particulars in them 'in a fair and legible manner'. These were:

1   A pledge book, which was to contain columns, headed as follows:
    Date of redemption
    Profit charged
    Amount of loan
    Number of pledges in the month
    Name of pawner
    Name of owner, if other than pawner
    Address of owner, if other than pawner
    List of articles pawned, as described on pawn ticket

*On the reasons for the Act, see pp. 70-2.

'All entries in the last five columns respecting each pledge shall be made on the day of the pawning thereof or within four hours after the end of that day.'

2 A pawn-ticket, the wording of which varied with the amount of the loan. On each type of ticket, however, there had to be entered the name and address of the pawnbroker and the pawner and a brief description of the article pawned, and all tickets ended with these two provisions:

'If the pledge is destroyed or damaged by fire the Pawnbroker will be bound to pay the value of the pledge, after deducting the amount of the loan and profit, such value to be the amount of the loan and profit and twenty-five per cent on the amount of the loan, unless otherwise agreed upon by the pawner and Pawnbroker.

'If this ticket is lost or mislaid the pawner should at once apply to the Pawnbroker for a form of declaration to be made before a magistrate, or the Pawnbroker will be bound to deliver the pledge to any person who produces this ticket to him and claims to redeem the same.'

The special wording, according to the category of loan, was:

A For loans of ten shillings or under:
'The Pawnbroker is entitled to charge –
'For this ticket   ..   ..   One halfpenny
'For profit on each two shillings or part of two shillings lent on this pledge for not more than one calendar month   ..   ..   One halfpenny
'And so on at the same rate per calendar month.
'After the first calendar month any time not exceeding fourteen days will be charged as half a month, and any time exceeding fourteen days and not more than one month will be charged as one month.

'This pledge must be redeemed within twelve calendar months and seven days from the date of pledging. At the end of that time it becomes the property of the Pawnbroker.'

B For loans of above ten shillings and not above forty shillings:

'*The Pawnbroker is entitled to charge

For this ticket   ..   ..   One penny

For profit on each two shillings or part of
two shillings lent on this pledge for not
more than one calendar month   ..   ..   One halfpenny
'And so on at the same rate per calendar
month.

'After the first calendar month any time not
exceeding fourteen days will be charged as
half a month, and any time exceeding
fourteen days and not more than one month
will be charged as one month.

'If this pledge is not redeemed within twelve calendar months
and seven days from the day of pledging, it may be sold by auction
by the Pawnbroker, but it may be redeemed at any time before the
day of sale.

'Within three years after sale the pawner may inspect the
account of the sale in the Pawnbroker's books on payment of one
penny, and receive any surplus produced by the sale. But deficit on
sale of one pledge may be set off by the Pawnbroker against surplus
on another.'

C   For loans of above forty shillings:

'*The Pawnbroker is entitled to charge

'For this ticket   ..   ..   One penny

'For profit on each two shillings and sixpence or part of two shillings and sixpence
lent on this pledge for every calendar month
or part of a calendar month   ..   ..   One halfpenny

'If this pledge is not redeemed within twelve calendar months
and seven days from the day of pledging, it may be sold by auction
by the Pawnbroker, but it may be redeemed at any time before the
day of sale.

'Within three years after sale the pawner may inspect the
account of the sale in the Pawnbroker's books on payment of one
penny, and receive any surplus produced by the sale. But deficit on

'* The following is to be printed on the ticket, on the front or back, or
partly on the front and partly on the back.'

sale of one pledge may be set off by the Pawnbroker against surplus on another.'

For more valuable goods, it was also possible to pawn by means of what was called a Special Contract. This had to be signed by both parties and included the same preliminaries and final clauses as the other tickets. The section relating to terms was different, however. It read as follows:

'The Pawnbroker charges
'For this ticket   ..   ..
'Profit at the rate per calendar month of ..
'After the first calendar month any time not exceeding fourteen days will be charged as half a month, and any time exceeding fourteen days and not more than one month will be charged as one month ..   ..   ..
'The charge for storage of this pledge will be   per calendar month, or any part of a month, in addition to the charges above mentioned.'

There were strict rules for the auctioning of all pledges of above ten shillings.

'1   The auctioneer shall cause all pledges to be exposed to public view.
'2   He shall publish catalogues of the pledges, stating –
      (a)   The Pawnbroker's name and place of business;
      (b)   The month in which each pledge was pawned;
      (c)   The number of each pledge as entered at the time of pawning in the pledge book.
'3   The pledges of each Pawnbroker in the catalogue shall be separate from any pledges of any other Pawnbroker.
'4   The auctioneer shall insert in some public newspaper an advertisement giving notice of the sale, and stating –
      (a)   The Pawnbroker's name and place of business;
      (b)   The months in which the pledges were pawned.
'5   The advertisement shall be inserted on two several days in the same newspaper, and the second advertisement shall be inserted at least three clear days before the first day of sale.
'6   Pictures, prints, books, bronzes, statues, busts, carvings in

153

ivory and marble, cameos, intaglios, musical, mathematical, and philosophical instruments, and china, sold by auction, shall be sold by themselves, and without any other goods being sold at the same sale, four times only in every year (that is to say,) on the first Monday in the months of January, April, July, and October, and on the following day and days, if the sale exceeds one day, and at no other time.

'7 Where a Pawnbroker bids at a sale the auctioneer shall not take the bidding in any other form than that in which he takes the biddings of other persons at the same sale; and the auctioneer on knocking down any article to a Pawnbroker shall forthwith declare audibly the name of the Pawnbroker as purchaser.

'8 The auctioneer shall, within fourteen days after the sale, deliver to the Pawnbroker a copy of the catalogue, or of so much thereof as relates to the pledges of that Pawnbroker, filled up with the amounts for which the several pledges of that Pawnbroker were sold, and authenticated by the signature of the auctioneer.

'9 The Pawnbroker shall preserve every such catalogue for three years at least after the auction.'

Every Pawnbroker had to be in possession of an annual licence, issued by the Commissioner of Inland Revenue and costing £7 10s. A separate licence was required for each shop. Persons applying for a licence for the first time were required to submit a certificate granted in the metropolitan police district by a magistrate and elsewhere by a justice at petty sessions specially convened for the purpose. Before making application for this certificate, he had to proceed as follows:

'1 Twenty-one days at least before the application he shall give notice by registered letter sent by post of his intention to one of the overseers of the poor of the parish or place in which he intends to carry on business, and to the superintendent of police of the district, and shall in the notice set forth his name and address:

'2 Within twenty-eight days before the application he shall cause a like notice to be affixed and maintained between ten o'clock in the morning and five o'clock in the afternoon of two consecutive Sundays, on the principal door or one of the doors of the church or chapel of the parish or place, or if there is none,

154

then on some other public and conspicuous place in the parish or place.'

Provided he had complied with these regulations, he was not to be refused a certificate unless he had failed to produce satisfactory evidence of good conduct or unless 'the shop in which he intends to carry on the business of a Pawnbroker, or any adjacent house or place occupied by him, is frequented by thieves or persons of bad character.'

A pawnbroker was subject to a number of other rules and regulations under the Act. Two of them related to public announcements on his premises.

'1 He shall always keep exhibited in large characters over the outer door of his shop his Christian name and surname or names, with the word Pawnbroker:

'2 He shall always keep placed in a conspicuous part of his shop (so as to be legible for every person pawning or redeeming pledges, standing in any box or place provided in the shop for persons pawning or redeeming pledges) the same information as is by the rules of the Third Schedule to this Act required to be printed on pawn tickets.'

There were certain general restrictions on his conduct. He was to be deemed guilty of an offence under the Act if he did any of the following things:

'1 Takes an article in pawn from any person appearing to be under the age of twelve years, or to be intoxicated:

'2 Purchases or takes in pawn or exchange a pawn-ticket issued by another Pawnbroker:

'3 Employs any servant or apprentice or other person under the age of sixteen years to take pledges in pawn:

'4 Carries on the business of a Pawnbroker on Sunday, Good Friday, or Christmas Day, or a day appointed for public fast, humiliation, or thanksgiving:

'5 Under any pretence purchases, except at public auction, any pledge while in pawn with him:

'6 Suffers any pledge while in pawn with him to be redeemed with a view to his purchasing it:

'7 Makes any contract or agreement with any person pawning or offering to pawn any article, or with the owner thereof, for the purchase, sale, or disposition thereof within the time of redemption:

'8 Sells or otherwise disposes of any pledge pawned with him except at such time and in such manner as authorised by this Act:'

A pawnbroker would also be contravening the Act if he 'knowingly takes in pawn any linen or apparel or unfinished goods or materials intrusted (sic) to any person to wash, scour, iron, mend, manufacture, work up, finish, or make up'.

Any stolen property found on a pawnbroker's premises was to be 'forthwith restored to the owner thereof', even if the pawnbroker had no reason to suppose it to be stolen when he accepted it as a pledge. The police, equipped with a warrant, were authorised to search a pawnbroker's shop 'within the hours of business'. 'If the Pawnbroker, on request by a constable authorised by the warrant, refuses to open the shop and permit it to be searched, a constable may break it open within the hours of business, and search as he thinks fit therein for the linen, apparel, goods, materials, or article aforesaid, doing no wilful damage; and if any Pawnbroker or other person opposes or hinders the search, he shall be guilty of an offence against this Act.'

And, as a final sanction, 'If a Pawnbroker is convicted on indictment of any fraud in his business, or of receiving stolen goods knowing them to be stolen, the court before which he is convicted may, if it thinks fit, direct that his licence shall cease to have effect, and the same shall so cease accordingly.'

Appendix 2

Past and Present Officers of the National Pawnbrokers' Association

PRESIDENTS

Alderman John Goolden, J.P., 1892–1895
Mr H. A. Attenborough, J.P., 1895–1913
Mr W. Bull, 1913–1925*
Mr Sidney Smith, 1925–1931*
Mr F. K. Ohlson, 1931–1940*
Mr James Smellie, 1940–1941
Mr A. E. Thomson, 1941–1946*
Mr Edgar Bowes, 1946–1949*
Mr W. H. Dawson, 1949–1958*
Mr W. J. D. Porritt, 1958–1966*
Mr A. D. Cook, 1966–1967
Mr E. T. Brown, 1968–1970*
Mr C. Suttenstall, 1970–1980*
Mr H. S. Wilkins, 1980

VICE-PRESIDENTS

Mr A. A. George, 1899–1901
Mr Stanley J. Attenborough, 1904–1910
Mr C. J. Thompson, 1910–1915
Mr R. H. Attenborough, 1916–1931*
Mr John Long, 1931–1937*
Mr James Smellie, 1937–1940
Mr Edgar Bowes, 1941–1946
Mr A. E. Thomson, 1946–1949
Mr W. R. Amos, 1949–1953*
Mr L. G. Norris, 1953–1958*
Mr E. T. Brown, 1958–1968

Mr C. Suttenstall, 1968–1970
Mr S. J. Davies, 1970–1972*
Mr H. S. Wilkins, 1972–1980
Mr J. D. G. Cook, 1980

TREASURERS

Mr J. Ashbridge Telfer, 1892–1895
Mr W. Bull, 1895–1913
Mr C. H. Bingemann, 1913–1931
Mr R. J. Starling, 1931–1941*
Mr W. R. Amos, 1941–1949
Mr L. G. Norris, 1949–1953
Mr E. T. Brown, 1953–1958
Mr S. J. Davies, 1958–1970
Mr H. S. Wilkins, 1970–1972
Mr F. E. Roberts, 1972

HONORARY SECRETARIES

Mr Alfred Hardaker, 1892–1895
Mr James Sprunt, 1895–1900
Mr C. J. Thompson, 1900–1910
Mr W. Bull *(pro. tem.)*, 1910–1912
Mr Sidney Smith, 1913–1921
Mr F. K. Ohlson, 1921–1931
Mr P. Davies, 1931–1937
Mr B. G. Paul, 1937–1941

GENERAL SECRETARIES

Mr B. G. Paul, 1941–1953
Mr J. E. Brown, 1953

ASSISTANT SECRETARIES

Mr John Attenborough, 1913–1926
Mr Charles A. Oak, 1925–1941
Mr J. E. Brown, 1949–1953

* Appointed Honorary Members of the Council.

Officers and Council, *1981/2*

BOOKS AND ARTICLES
RELATING TO PAWNBROKING

Pawnbroking in general
Bentham, Jeremy, *A Defence of Usury*, London: T. Payne & Son, 1787. 3rd ed. 1816.
Hardaker, Alfred, *A Brief History of Pawnbroking*, London: Jackson, Ruston and Keeson, 1892.
Levine, S. W., *The Business of Pawnbroking*, New York, 1913.
Mayfield, J. W., *Sidelights on Pawnbroking*, Hull: privately printed, 1912.
Minkes, A. L., 'The Decline of Pawnbroking', *Economica*, February 1953.
'My Uncle', *All the Year Round*, n.s., vol. XXXVII, 1885–6, pp. 245–51.
National Pawnbrokers' Association, 'Official Souvenir of the Eleventh Triennial Meeting, Bristol, 1928', *The Pawnbrokers' Gazette*, 1928.
'A Pawnbroker', *An Apology for the Business of Pawnbroking*, London 1744. Reprinted 1859.
'A Pawnbroker', *A Few Words on Pawnbroking, &c*, London: Jackson, Ruston and Keeson, 1866.
'Pawnbroking', *Quarterly Review*, vol. CLV, 1883, pp. 106–33.
'Pawnbroking Establishments in England and on the Continent', *The Penny Magazine*, 29 October 1836, pp. 423–4.
Pawnbroker's Guide, with Digest of Laws, London: Washbourne, 1856.

The law relating to pawnbroking
Attenborough, Charles L., *The Law Affecting Pawnbroking*, London: Jackson, Ruston and Keeson, 1905.
Levine, S. W., *A Treatise on the Law of Pawnbroking . . . and a Review of Pawnbroking*, New York, 1911.
Report of the Commissioner Appointed to Inquire into the Laws of Pawnbroking in Ireland, Parliament, Sessional Papers, 1867, vol. XXXII, No. 3985. Dublin, 1868.

Pawnbroking in its social context
Macrae, David, jr. *The Social Hydra : or, the Influences of the Traffic of Pawnbrokers and Brokers on the Religious, Moral and Social*

Conditions of the Working Classes and the Poor, Glasgow: George Gallie, 1861.

Mayhew, Henry, *London Labour and the London Poor*, Vols. II and IV, 1861–2. Reprinted 1968 by Dover Publications.

Roberts, Robert, *The Classic Slum*, Harmondsworth: Penguin, 1973.

Stevenson, John, *Social Conditions in Britain between the Wars*, Harmondsworth: Penguin, 1977.

Pawnbroking in London

Booth, Charles, *Life and Labour of the People in London*, Vol. II. 4th ed. London: Macmillan, 1902.

Keeson, C. A. Cuthbert, 'Pawnbroking London', in *Living London* (ed. George R. Sims), Vol. II, pp. 36–42. London: Cassell, 1906.

Price, F. G. Hilton, 'Some notes upon the Signs of the Pawnbrokers in London in the Seventeenth and Eighteenth Centuries', *Archaeological Journal*, Vol. LIX, No. 234, pp. 160–200. London: Harrison & Sons, 1902.

Pawnbroking in the North-East

Callaghan, Thomas, *A Lang Way to the Pa'nshop*, Newcastle: Frank Graham. Undated, but from internal evidence, c.1979.

Stabler, Arthur, *Ganning along the Scotswood Road*: a social history of the Scotswood Road community from 1847. Paper read at the meeting of the British Association, Lancaster, 1976. Typescript in Newcastle Central Library.

Pawnbroking in Scotland

Malcolm, Robert, *An Exposure of the Wee Pawn System*, Glasgow: Malcolm, 1850.

Scouller, Edward, 'Uncle Limited, Glasgow', *Scotland*, January 1948.

Weir, William, *The First Hundred Years, 1851–1951: a sketch of the history of the Glasgow Pawnbrokers' Association*, Glasgow: A. Duncan & Son, 1951.

Pawnbroking in Ireland

Dalton, Martin, 'Monday is Pawnday', *The Bell*, Vol. XIV, No. 1, April 1947.

O'Donnell, Peadar, 'People and Pawnshops', *The Bell*, Vol. V, No. 1, October 1942.

'On the Mont de Piété System of Pawnbroking in Ireland', *Journal of the Statistical Society of London*, Vol. III, 1840–1, pp. 293–303.

'Pawnbroking in Ireland', *Dublin University Magazine*, Vol. XIV, 1839.

Raymond, R. J., 'Pawnbrokers and Pawnbroking in Dublin, 1830–70', *Dublin Historical Record*, Vol. XXXII, No. 1, December 1978.

Aberdeen Loan Company, 89
Ackroyd, S. R., 109
Adams, Police-constable, 49
*Address to the Inhabitants of
   Limerick*, 40
Adgey, Bob, 104
Allen, Samuel, 102
Allsopp, Charles, 77–9
almshouses, 51
Antwerp, 26
Ashford, Mr, 56
assistant pawnbrokers, 46–7,
   57–8, 66, 67, 75–85, 92, 94,
   101, 102–5, 111, 112, 125, 134
Attenborough, H. A., 72
Attenborough, Richard, 61
Attenborough's, pawnbrokers,
   56, 61
auctioneers, 37, 39, 153
auction pledges, 139
auctions, 37, 39, 152, 153
Aymas, Mr, pawnbroker, 64

Baker, J. B. H., 77, 78, 106–7
bank loans, 10
bankruptcy, 47
banks, 147
Barnett, S., 93
Barran, Sir John, 68
Barrington, Matthew, 39
Bath, 110, 134
Bath Directory, 47
Batley, 67
Battersea Dogs' Home, 117
Belfast, 91, 101, 102, 103–4
Belfast Pawnbrokers' Association,
   121
Benevolent Association of Assistant
   Pawnbrokers, 69, 93–4
Bentwick, 69
Berwick-on-Tweed, 29

billiard balls, 68
Bingham, John, 103
binoculars – as pledges, 104
Birkbeck, Alderman, 55
Birkenhead, 72, 73
Birmingham, 66, 110, 145
Birmingham and District
   Pawnbrokers' Benevolent
   Association, 110
Birmingham Pawnbrokers'
   Association, 88, 121
Blackburn, 110
Board of Guardians, 105
Boer War, 90
Bolton, 70
Bolton and District Pawnbrokers'
   Association, 121
Bootle, 115
Boulton, Mr, pawnbroker, 72
Bowes, David, 55, 146
Bowes, James, 54–5, 108
Bowes, John, 54
Bradford, 127
Bradford Chamber of Trade, 109
Bradford Pawnbrokers'
   Association, 109
Brereton, Jack, 146
Brereton, J. B., 146–7
Brief History of Pawnbroking, A,
   18
Bristol, 55, 75–8, 106–7, 110
Bristol City Council, 111
Bristol and District Pawnbrokers'
   Association, 122
British Association, 44, 45
Broadmead Baptist Chapel, 111
Brown, Edwin T., 55
Browne, Dr, Member of the Dail,
   131
Bruges, 26
Bull, Horace, 125

Bull, Walter, 72, 87, 107–9, 125
Business of Pawnbroking, The, 18
Butler, John Judkin, 39

Cadogan, Lady Honoria, 61
Cadogan, Lord, 61
Cahors, 24
Cahorsins, 24, 26
cameras – as pledges, 140
Cameron, William, 54
canary – as pledge, 70
Canterbury, 72
capital, 67
Cardiff, 90, 93
catalogues – of auctions, 154
Census – of 1851, 53
Chamberlain, Mrs, 128–9
Charles the Bold, 26
Charitable Corporation, 32
Charitable Pawn Office, 39–40
Charitable Pawn Offices (Ireland)
    Act (1842), 140
charitable pawnshops, 28
charters – regulating pawnbroking,
    27
children, 155
Children's Bill, 115
China, 22
Christina, 92
Church – and usury, 23, 25
churchmen – as pledges, 27
Church of Scotland, 54
Clarkson, Joseph, 109–10
Clayton, Elizabeth, 65–6
Clears, Mr, pawnbroker, 94
Cleland, Dr, 44
Clerkenwell Police Court, 65
clothing, 59, 60, 70, 78, 85–6, 113,
    128, 140
coal vouchers, 105
Colburn, John, 72
Cole, G. D. H., 16
Coleman, Joseph, Ltd., 94
Collins, James, Ltd., 110
Collins, Thomas, 64
Cologne, 26
Colquhoun, Patric, 41, 42
commercial travellers, 70

Common Council of London, 32
Common People, The, 16
computers, 142
Conan Doyle, Sir Arthur, 52,
    144–5
concerts, 69
Consumer Credit Act (1974), 35,
    71, 139, 140–2
Consumer Credit Committee,
    139–40
contributions – to National
    Pawnbrokers' Association, 72
Cooke, Mr, pawnbroker, 72
Cork, 91
corporate companies, 89
councillors – pawnbrokers as, 47,
    54, 72
Coventry, 67–8
Crewe, 111–12
criminals, 48–51
Crooke, Sir J. Smedley, 145
crowns – as pledges, 27
Croydon, 105
cubicles, 85, 147
Currie, Robert, 110
Customs and Excise Reports, 122

Daily Mail, 113
Danes, 22
Dante, 26
Davis, Thomas, 66
Delfau, Mr, of Paris, 117
Derby, 71
Derby, Earl of, 27
Desart, Lord, 64
Dickens, Charles, 18–19, 145
Dickens Fellowship, 110
Dicker and Scarlett, 56
dinners, 69
Director-General of Fair
    Trading, 140
dole, 97
dolly-shops, 60
Dowling, Mr Commissioner, 50
*Down and Out in Paris and
    London,* 16
Dublin, 39, 47, 91, 130, 143, 146
Dublin, Marshal of, 36–7, 39

Earp, Kathleen, 127–8
Eaton, J. D., 110
Ebbw Vale, 79
Edinburgh, 124
*Edinburgh and Leith Post Office
  Directory*, 101
Edward I, 24
Edward III, 26
Edwards, Harry, 68
Elliott, Mr, magistrate, 64–5
English Social History, 13–14
Enshaw, Mrs, 50
Equitable Loan Company of
  Scotland, 101
Every Man in His Humour, 29
Excise licence, 35

false teeth – as pledge, 67, 103
Family Means Test, 97
Fayerbrother, W. M., 57, 58
Fileman, Mr, 56
Finlay, Moses, 101
Fish Bros., 56
Fish, Charles, 57–8
Fish, P. W., 56
Flemming, Mr, pawnbroker, 49
Florentines, 14
Fowler, Mr, pawnbroker's
  manager, 81
Fox, Mr, pawnbroker, 115
France, 44–5
Franciscans, 28
Fraser, Mr, pawnbroker, 72
fraud, 48, 63–4, 156
Freemasonry, 55, 91, 107
French Ministry of Commerce, 44
furs – as pledges, 140
Futurist, 110

Gateshead, 79–80
General Medical Council, 65
George III, 36
George V, 55
Gin Lane, 14–15
Glasgow, 44, 53–4, 112, 113, 125
Glasgow Protective Association,
  89, 121
Golders Green, 143–4, 146

Goldschmidt & Weisman, of
  Berlin, 117
goldsmiths, 14, 32
Goldsmiths' and General Burglary
  Insurance Association, 72
Gomm, G. F., 94
Goolden, John, 72, 91
Gorman, P., 112
Gowland, Mr, solicitor, 66
Great Depression, 97
Great Exhibition, 53
Great Western Cotton Mill,
  Bristol, 76
Greer, Ann, 67
Grimsby, 145
grocery vouchers, 105
guns – as pledges, 104
Guy, Count of Flanders, 26

Haigh, David, 134
Halton and District Institute, 111
Hanley, 72
Hardaker, Alfred, 9, 17, 59, 71, 72
Harpurhey, 90–1
Hart, Mr, pawnbroker, 72
Harvey & Thompson, 56, 81–2,
  133–4, 143–5, 146
Haughey, Charles, 130–2
Hawes, Mr, 56
Hayes, Professor, 131–2
Henry III, 25
Hill Bros., 101
Hill, William, 101
hire purchase, 113
His Last Bow, 52
Hogarth, William, 14
Holborn Restaurant, London, 69
Holmes, Sherlock, 52
Honourable Artillery Company,
  125
hours, 75, 77, 102, 103
household ornaments, 55
Hull, 115
Hush, Ernest, 104, 129
Hutchinson, Henry, 54
Hyde, Mr, pawnbroker, 115

ice-cream sellers – in Belfast, 104

Ilkeston, 110
Ilkley, 68
illegal pawnbroking, 37, 60
Illustrated London News, The, 47,
    49–51
image – of pawnbroking, 134,
    135, 145, 146
incomes – of pawnbrokers, 37–8
Industrial Revolution, 31
infectious diseases, 70
insurance, 72
interest rates, 28, 32, 35, 36, 40,
    41, 60, 88, 104, 129, 152–3
intoxication, 155
Ipswich, 72
IRA, 102
Ireland, 35–40
Irish Pawnbrokers' Act (1786),
    36–7
Irish Pawnbrokers' Act (1788),
    36–7
Irish Pawnbrokers' Act (1843), 39
Irish Pawnbrokers' Bill (1964), 130
'Is Pawnbroking on the Decline?',
    88
Italian city republics, 25
Italian community – in Belfast,
    103–4

Jackson, J. T., 68
Jacobs, Sammy, 106
James II, 32
jewellery, 27, 30, 52, 58, 61–3, 64,
    66, 79, 81, 82, 90, 91, 104,
    115–16, 125, 128, 140, 146, 147
Jews, 14, 24, 25, 31, 39, 93, 100–1,
    106
Johnson, Charles, 48
Jonson, Ben, 29
Justices of the Peace –
    pawnbrokers as, 47, 91, 92

Kent, 113
Kidd, Mrs E. P., 79–80
Knapp, Walter, 93–4

Lancashire, 90
laundry, 156

Leeds, 68, 111
Leeds Assistants' Association, 110
Leeds Chamber of Trades, 111
Leeds Credit Retailers'
    Association, 111
Leeds Pawnbrokers'
    Association, 121
legal regulations, 27
Leicester, 94
Leicester and Leicestershire
    Pawnbrokers' Association, 121
Levine, S. W., 18
Liberal Party, 55
licences, 123, 128, 154–5
'Life Among the Pledges', 83–5
Limerick, 39–40
Limited Liabilities Companies
    Acts, 89
Liquor Control Board, 87
Lisburn, 126
Liverpool, 50, 59, 98, 105, 106,
    110, 115
Liverpool, Birkenhead and
    District Pawnbrokers'
    Protection Society, 121
living-in, 81, 83, 94
local government – pawnbrokers
    in, 47, 54, 72, 73, 76, 91, 111
Lombard House, London, 107–8,
    132–3
Lombards, 24, 25, 32
London, 42, 49–51, 53, 55–7,
    61–4, 65–7, 80–5, 93–4, 113–14,
    143
London Jewellers Ltd., 115–16
*London Labour and the London
    Poor*, 59–60
London School of Economics, 134
Lord Chancellor, 92
Lord Lieutenant of Dublin, 37
'Lord Nelson', Bristol, 78–9
Louvain, 27
Lowenburg, Mr, pawnbroker, 66
low pledges, 139
Lucombe, A. C., 134
Lurgan, Lord, 104
Lynn, H. A., 103
Lyon, Council of, 23, 24

Mackay, Watson, 54
magistrates – pawnbrokers as, 47,
    72, 91, 92, 145
Maguire, T., 57
*Making of the English Working
    Class, The*, 16
Malines, 27
Manchester, 54–5, 90–1, 110
Manchester Grammar School,
    54–5
Manchester Pawnbrokers' Bowling
    Club, 110
Manchester and Salford
    Cooperative Society, 54
Manchester, Salford and District
    Pawnbrokers' Protection
    Society, 121
Manchester Ship Canal, 55
Manchester Trams Committee, 55
Manchester Union Glee Club, 55
Marshal of Dublin, 36, 37, 39
Martin, Thomas G., 102–3
Mayhew, Henry, 59–60
mayors – pawnbrokers as, 72, 76,
    91, 111, 145
McKeown, Mr, pawnbroker,
    103–4
McNally, Jim, 126–7
Medici family, 33
Medici states, 24
Members of Parliament –
    pawnbrokers as, 76, 111, 145
men's outfitting, 55
Meston, Lord, 130
Metropolitan Pawnbrokers'
    Protection Society, 72, 121, 133
Mexborough, 105, 134
Meyrick, Lloyd, 93
middle class – as pawnbrokers'
    customers, 124
Middlesbrough, 105, 129
Middlesbrough, Stockton and
    District Pawnbrokers'
    Association, 121
Millar, J. S., 125
Minkes, A. L., 134, 138–9
Mobbs, G. H., 80–1
Moberley, L. G., 92

moneychangers, 24
moneylenders, 14, 22, 23, 24, 105,
    122, 129, 139
Moneylenders' Act (Northern
    Ireland) (1933), 140
montes pietatis, 28, 32
monts de piété, 40
Moore, W. H., Ltd., 134
Morritt, Mr, of Westminster, 48
mortgages, 10
Mouilliett, Louis, 64
Murphy, Philip, 144–5, 146
Murphy, Senator, 131
Murray, Col., 104
Murray, Edmund, 104
musical instruments – as pledges,
    83, 103, 104, 140
'mystery gold', 64

National Pawnbrokers'
    Association, 11–12, 53, 71–2,
    87, 92, 107, 110, 121, 129–30,
    132, 139, 145
National Union of Assistant
    Pawnbrokers, 94
Netherlands, 26
Newcastle upon Tyne, 69, 72,
    91–2, 99–100, 105, 134, 146
Newcastle City Council, 91
Newcastle, Gateshead and District
    Pawnbrokers' Association, 121
New Cross, 82
Newport, South Wales, 106
Nixon, Alderman Tom, 91
noblemen – as pledges, 27
NOP Market Research, Ltd., 139
Northampton, Earl of, 27
North Staffordshire Pawnbrokers'
    Association, 121
Norwich, 145
Notre Dame, Paris, 23
Nottingham, 111
Nottingham and District
    Pawnbrokers' Association, 121
NPA Journal, 132, 134
Nugent, Joseph, 103–4

Observant Friars, 28

officers – pawnbrokers as, 125
opening hours, 130
Orpington, 133
Orwell, George, 16–17
Ottaway, T. J., 80
Oxford English Dictionary, 30

Page, Sir Graham, 130
Papacy, 23, 24, 26
Paris, 44, 45
Paris, Bishop of, 23
Parker, W. H., 128
Parker, W. J., 128
Parkin, Richard, 59
Parliamentary Inquiries, 15
Parritt, Mr, pawnbroker, 69–70
Parry, John, 50
Pawnbrokers' Act (1784), 35
Pawnbrokers' Act (1800), 35
Pawnbrokers' Act (1872), 35, 53,
    58, 70–1, 114, 129, 150–6
Pawnbrokers' Act (Northern
    Ireland) (1954), 140
Pawnbrokers' Act (1960), 129, 140
pawnbrokers' assistants, 46–7,
    57–8, 66, 67, 75–85, 92, 94,
    101, 102–5, 111, 112, 125, 126,
    134
Pawnbrokers' Charitable
    Institution, 51, 133
Pawnbrokers' Gazette, The, 53,
    67, 68, 69, 72–3, 87–8, 89–90,
    92–3, 107–8, 125, 132
Pawnbrokers' General Council, 91
pawnbrokers' licences, 123, 128,
    154–6
pawnbrokers' protection
    associations, 71, 121–2
Pawnbrokers' Protection Society –
    of Glasgow, 53, 54; of London,
    66
pawnbrokers' signs, 33, 115, 123
Pawnbroking Parliamentary
    Reform Association, 59
Pawning Industrial Tools Bill, 115
pawnshop – used as cloakroom, 70
'Pawnshop and Tallyman', 85–6
pawn tickets, 80, 151–3

Penny Magazine, 45, 46
Pepys, Samuel, 30, 32
Perth, 112
Perth Loan Company, 112
Peterborough, Lady, 30, 32
Pill, 106
plate, 61, 82, 104
pledging-boxes, 85, 147
Plymouth, 106, 113
Pocklington, C. R., 134
police, 156
police charities, 100
Poor Relief, 105
population, 31–2
porcelain, 146, 147
Porritt's, of Newcastle, 146
*Portraits of Eminent
    Conservatives*, 64
Portsmouth, Southsea and
    Landport Pawnbrokers'
    Association, 122
port wine, 64
postal pawning, 125
Postgate, Raymond, 16
Post Office Directory, 100
Presidential Badge – of the
    National Pawnbrokers'
    Association, 109
Priestley, J. B., 17
priests, 23
profiles of pawnbrokers – in the
    Gazette, 73
profits, 40, 58, 88, 123, 124, 130,
    137–8
public holidays, 155

Quakers, 14
Quin, J. D., 124–5

Radcliffe, A., 73
radios – as pledges, 140
Raselle's, of Bristol, 55
Raymond, R. J., 38, 40, 47
razors – as pledges, 103
Reeves, Mr, 56
religious ornaments – as pledges,
    27
Rendle, H. G., 106

restrictions – on pawnbrokers, 155–6
Richardson, Mr, of Cannes, 117
rings – as pledges, 98, 105
Robertson's, Messrs., 116
Rochester, 72
Rogers, Mr, pawnbroker, 104
Roman Catholics, 39, 106
Romans, 22
Romford, 69
Rose, Mrs, jeweller, 49
Rotherham, 110
Royal Commission on the Selection of JPs, 92
Royal Commissions, 15
Rushton, Mr, JP, 50

Salford, 73
Samuel, L. P., 110
sashes – as pledges, 103
Saunders, Betty, 81–2
Saxons, 22
Scala, Ltd., 110
Scotland, 147
Scotswood Road, Newcastle upon Tyne, 99–100
securities – given by pawnbrokers, 36, 37
Select Committees on pawnbroking, 59, 71
servants, 61
Shakespeare, William, 29
Sharp, John, 116–17
Shaw, Joe, 102
Shaw, J. J., 145
Shaw, Mr, pawnbroker, 72
Sheffield, 91, 110, 128
Sheffield Billposting Company, 91
Sheffield City Council, 91
Sheffield Crimean and Indian Mutiny Veterans' Association, 91
Sheffield, Rotherham and District Pawnbrokers' Association, 121
Sheffield Wednesday Football Club, 91
Sheward, William, 145
Ship Hotel, Wigan, 69

shoplifting, 49–51
Sketches by Boz, 18–19
slums, 100
Smetham, Henry, 110
Smith, Charles, 106
Smith, Sidney, 108
Smith, William, 48
Sneinton, 111
social activities, 68–9
social security, 10
soft furnishings, 55
Southend-on-Sea, 133
Southport, 73
special contracts, 71, 139, 153
specialisation – among Belfast pawnbrokers, 104
sports equipment – as pledges, 140
Sprunt, James, 72
Starr, Alderman and Mrs, 68
St Nicholas, 109
Stoke-on-Trent, 72
stolen goods, 48–51, 60–1, 145, 146
Stony Stratford, 29
Strasbourg, 44
Suttenstall, C., 134
Sutton, T. M., 116–7
Swaish, Sir John, 76, 111
Swift, Mr Justice, 116
Sykes, C. E., 111

tallymen, 85, 86
tape-recorders – as pledges, 140
Tawney, R. H., 23
tax – on Irish pawnbrokers, 130
telescope – as pledge, 69–70
television, 146
Thames Police Court, 66
Third Lateran Council, 23
Thom's Directory, 101
Thompson, Charles, 67
Thompson, E. P., 16
Thompson, James, 73
Thomson, Douglas, 56
Three Balls sign, 33, 115, 123
tiaras, 116–7
ticket-writing, 94, 102
ticket-writing machines, 80
Till, Mrs, 64–5

Times, The, 41–3, 47–8, 58–9, 62–3, 82–6, 87, 122–3
tools – as pledges, 104
training, 95
Treatise on Indigence, 41
Tremayne, Arthur, 95
Trevelyan, G. M., 13–15
Trier, 26

Ulster Volunteers, 104
'Uncle', 13, 73, 86, 128
unemployment, 97, 113
Unemployment Insurance, 97
unlicensed pawnbrokers, 37, 60; Irish Act against, 36
usurers, 23
usury, 23

'Vanishing Pawnbrokers', 122–3
Victoria, Queen, 57
Vienna, Council of, 23
vouchers – for coal and groceries, 105

wages, 57, 78, 79–81, 102, 103
Waller, Lewis, 115–6
Wall Street Crash, of 1929, 97

Wardle, Police-constable, 50
Warrington, William, 54
Waterston, John, 89, 112
Wells, Miss, 50
Welfare State, 9, 101, 122, 123, 124, 127
West Bromwich, 145
Wheeler, Sir Mortimer, 145
White, Jesse, 75–8
Whiting, John, 111
Wigan Pawnbrokers' Association, 69
Wigan Pier, The Road to, 16
William the Conqueror, 24
Williamson, James & Sons, 101
Willis, Mr, pawnbroker, 72
Wilson, F., 69
Wilson, Jabez, 145
Windsor, Emile, 111–12
Womersley, Sir Walter, 145
Woolwich, 82
Worcester, 94
workhouse, 65
Worship Street Police Court, 65
Wort, S. E., 125
Wright, John, 61

York, 72